JAMES MARTIN

PHOTOGRAPHY BY YUKI SUGIURA

HOME COMFORTS

Thanks to all of you reading this bit, for watching the shows and for helping my dreams come true. And for that I can never thank you enough.

Publishing director: Jane O'Shea
Creative director: Helen Lewis
Art direction and design: Gabriella Le Grazie
Photographer: Yuki Sugiura
Project editor: Lucy Bannell
Food stylists: Janet Brinkworth, David Birt, Chris Start...
  and James Martin
Props stylist: Rebecca Newport
Home economist: Janet Brinkworth
Production controller: Tom Moore
Production director: Vincent Smith

First published in 2014 by
Quadrille Publishing Limited
www.quadrille.co.uk

Text © 2014 James Martin
Photography © 2014 Yuki Sugiura
Design and layout © 2014 Quadrille Publishing Limited

Cataloguing in Publication Data: a catalogue record for
this book is available from the British Library.

978 1 84949 472 4
Printed in Italy

Contents

I've been doing this job for 20 years now and never have I had such an amazing response to an idea and a show as I have with Home Comforts.

I think that's because, like most of us, I work harder now than I've ever done, with longer hours and more stress. And after all those long days, there is nothing that I like more than chilling out at home with some delicious, comforting food. I don't mean what we traditionally call 'comfort food', such as pie and mash or rib-sticking steamed puddings with custard (though those are here, too); to me, comforting food can just as easily be a beautifully made and cleverly dressed salad, a magnificent fish with a piquant salsa verde or a fresh raspberry and vodka jelly.

I've been very lucky to travel the world with my job, learning more about food, but there truly is no place like home. The UK is a very special place and I only realised that when I was seeing less of it. So to do a show based at home seemed an obvious thing to do. And it made my dogs happy, not only to have me around more, but also because – as they bounced around during the filming of the TV show and then afterwards in the photoshoot for this book – they got to hoover up the bits and bobs of food that fell off the tables… So they, like me, have really loved putting the book together!

Here are the recipes I love to cook at home. The ones I turn to when away from the restaurant and from TV studios. These are all the things I've learned over my career, coupled with some new recipes inspired by local producers and suppliers. And what amazing people we have met along the way, from cordial brewers to pork farmers and fabulous cheese makers. We should all look and see what is on our doorstep, there's plenty of delicious stuff for us all to discover.

This is a project I should have done ages ago. It's all about the food and working with food for as long as I have makes you understand it a little more. It makes you enjoy it more, too. And most importantly of all, it makes you crave that moment when you arrive home and get into the kitchen. We could all do with more home comforts. I hope you love these recipes as much as I do.

James

Introduction

Lighter comforts

Sometimes when I get home from work a quick light supper is all I crave. I have taken advantage of my veg garden for a few things in here, as I did on the TV show, but of course you can buy all the stuff from the supermarket. There are some great salad ideas and dressings that will bring any meal to life.

QUICK TOMATO AND BASIL SOUP WITH ROASTED GARLIC BREAD

San Marzano are the best canned tomatoes I know; they are sweet and have fewer seeds. I use them for pizza sauce, too. You will find them in the supermarket if you read the label. And making your own butter is nothing new… well, not to me anyway. Roasting the garlic softens it and turns this into the best garlic bread out there.

Making butter really is very easy and it is a great way to use up leftover double cream. It freezes well, too.

Serves 2 – 4

1 garlic bulb
500ml double cream
sea salt and freshly ground black pepper
leaves from a large bunch of basil, roughly chopped, 2 sprigs reserved
75ml extra virgin olive oil
½ banana shallot, finely chopped
2 x 400g cans of San Marzano tomatoes
1 small baguette, halved lengthways, then halved widthways

Preheat the oven to 180°C/350°F/gas mark 4. Wrap the whole garlic bulb in foil then place on a baking tray and roast for 40–45 minutes until soft. Set aside until cool enough to handle, then cut the top off of the bulb, squeeze out all the soft garlic and finely chop it.

Pour the double cream into the bowl of a food mixer and beat for three to five minutes until the mixture turns into solid lumps with a liquid base. You have made butter!

Tip out into a muslin or cloth-lined colander over a large bowl, wrap the muslin tightly around it and squeeze out all the liquid so that you have a solid mass of butter in the muslin, then discard the liquid.

Return the butter to the bowl, add the roast garlic and a generous pinch of salt, then stir in one-third of the chopped basil and mix once more.

Heat a large sauté pan until hot, add all but 2 tbsp of the extra virgin olive oil and the shallot and cook without colour for one minute. Add the canned tomatoes and the remaining basil (except the 2 reserved sprigs), then simmer for two or three minutes.

Meanwhile, heat a griddle pan until very hot and char the bread on both sides. Slather with the garlic butter and keep warm in a low oven.

Blitz the soup with a stick blender – or place in a blender and blitz – to a fine purée. If using a blender, make sure to fill it only one-third full. (You will probably have to blend the soup in batches.) Season with salt and pepper. You'll know your blender better than I do, but you need to make sure the centre part of the lid is slightly ajar, or it can create a vacuum which can pop the lid off and spray hot soup around the kitchen. Be careful.

Serve the soup in bowls with some of the reserved olive oil drizzled over the top and a scattering of shredded basil leaves from the reserved sprigs, with the garlic bread alongside.

SUMMER VEG SOUP WITH MUSSELS AND SALSA VERDE

This comes straight from my garden and into the bowl (except for the mussels!) and when the summer's in full swing in the veg garden there are few better soups. Add the salsa at the end to keep all the flavour and colour or, better still, let your guests add as much as they need.

Serves 4

For the soup
50g unsalted butter
1 banana shallot, finely chopped
150g courgettes, cut into 1cm cubes
1 fennel bulb, cut into 1cm cubes, fronds reserved
150g carrots, peeled and cut into 1cm cubes
100g celery sticks, cut into 1cm cubes
8 radishes, halved lengthways
500g mussels, scrubbed, beards removed (see page 134)
150ml white wine
750ml vegetable stock

For the salsa verde
2 tbsp roughly chopped mint leaves
2 tbsp roughly chopped dill fronds
2 tbsp roughly chopped tarragon leaves
2 tbsp roughly chopped flat-leaf parsley leaves
2 tbsp roughly chopped watercress leaves
2 tbsp torn basil leaves
1 large shallot, roughly chopped
6 anchovies, roughly chopped
2 tbsp capers, drained and rinsed
juice of ½ lemon
1 tsp Dijon mustard
4 tbsp extra virgin olive oil, plus more to store, if needed

Heat a sauté pan until medium hot, add the butter and all the vegetables and sweat over a low heat until just softened, about five minutes.

Add the mussels, wine and stock and bring to the boil, then cover and simmer for two or three minutes until all the mussels have opened. Discard any that fail to open.

Meanwhile, make the salsa verde. Place all the chopped herbs into a food processor and blitz to roughly chop, then add the shallot, anchovies, capers, lemon juice, mustard and oil and blitz to a slightly chunky purée. Season with salt and pepper.

Remove the soup from the heat, then stir 2–3 tbsp of salsa verde in, check the seasoning and serve immediately, with the rest of the salsa on the side.

Any leftover salsa verde should be decanted into a sealable container, covered with a thin layer of oil and kept in the fridge for up to four days.

Lighter Comforts 13

BUTTERNUT SQUASH SOUP WITH FLOWERPOT BREAD

I first made this while working on menus for the NHS. Butternut squash is packed full of flavour and the soup takes little time to make. The bread comes from a ready mix my mum uses and the idea of baking it in flowerpots is not new, but it just makes a fun way of presenting rolls.

I love these as they look great on the table. If there is space in your oven you can use a larger pot, too, to make a loaf.

Serves 4

450g packet ready-made pain de campagne bread mix

25g unsalted butter, plus more for the flowerpots

1 tbsp olive oil

½ onion, thinly sliced

450g butternut squash, peeled and cut into 1cm pieces

500ml vegetable stock

375ml milk

sea salt and freshly ground black pepper

finely grated zest and juice of 2 limes

Make the bread dough according to the packet instructions, then leave to prove in a large bowl in a warm place for one hour, or until doubled in size. Meanwhile, clean four small clay flowerpots, butter them and line with twists or strips of double-sided silicone kitchen paper.

Take the dough out and knock it back, then divide into four and place into the flowerpots. Leave to prove again for 30 minutes.

Preheat the oven to 220°C/425°F/gas mark 7. Place the flowerpots on a baking tray in the oven and bake for 10–15 minutes until golden brown and cooked through.

Meanwhile, heat the remaining butter and olive oil in a large saucepan or sauté pan, add the onion, cover and cook without colour for three or four minutes. Add the butternut squash and sauté for two or three minutes, then add all the remaining ingredients except the lime zest and juice.

Bring to the boil, then reduce the heat to a simmer and cook for six minutes, or until the butternut squash is cooked.

Pour into a blender, making sure to fill it only one-third full, cover with the lid and blitz to a purée. (You will probably have to blend the soup in batches.) You'll know your blender better than I do, but you need to make sure the centre part of the lid is slightly ajar, or it can create a vacuum which can pop the lid off and spray hot soup around the kitchen. Be careful.

Return the soup to the saucepan to heat through, then adjust the seasoning and finish with the lime zest and juice. Serve the soup with the flowerpot bread alongside.

SWEETCORN SOUP
WITH CRAB AND
HOME-SOURED CREAM

A lovely simple soup that can be made with either white or brown crab meat. The brown crab meat version will be richer and the white crab meat a little lighter. Or you can, of course, use a mixture of both. You can also use canned or frozen sweetcorn, so you can make this soup all year round.

Serves 4

25g unsalted butter
1 banana shallot, finely sliced
½ tsp curry powder
340g can of sweetcorn, or frozen sweetcorn
75ml white wine
200ml double cream
sea salt and freshly ground black pepper
juice of 1 lemon
100g picked white or brown crab meat,
    or a mixture
a little rapeseed oil, to serve

Heat a saucepan until medium hot, add the butter, shallot and curry powder and cook without colour for two or three minutes until the shallot has just softened.

Add the sweetcorn (and all the liquid from the can, if you're using canned), then add the wine and enough water to just cover.

Bring to a simmer, add half the cream, then season with salt and pepper.

Pour into a blender, making sure to fill it only one-third full, cover with the lid and blitz to a purée. (You will probably have to blend the soup in batches.) You'll know your blender better than I do, but you need to make sure the centre part of the lid is slightly ajar, or it can create a vacuum which can pop the lid off and spray hot soup around the kitchen. Be careful.

Return the soup to the pan and heat through gently, adding a squeeze of lemon juice, salt and pepper to taste.

Pour the remaining cream into a bowl with the remaining lemon juice then whisk until thickened (this is home-made soured cream!). Season with salt.

Ladle the soup into serving bowls, then top with a little of the crab, a spoonful of the soured cream and a drizzle of rapeseed oil.

The main thing about this soup is not to overcook it once you add the peas, or it will end up muddying the clean flavour you are after and tasting like mushy peas from a chippy.

Serves 4

For the ham hock

1 small ham hock, about 1kg
1 large onion, thickly sliced
1 shallot, thickly sliced
1 garlic bulb, halved horizontally
2 carrots, cut into chunks
1 celery stick, cut into chunks
3 sprigs of parsley
1 sprig of thyme
1 bay leaf
small handful of peppercorns

For the soup

25g unsalted butter
400g frozen peas
1 large bunch of flat-leaf parsley,
  roughly chopped
150ml double cream, plus more to serve
sea salt and freshly ground black pepper
2 tbsp rapeseed oil
1 long baguette, halved lengthways,
  then halved widthways
2 garlic cloves, halved

Place the ham hock into a deep saucepan, add the vegetables, herbs and peppercorns and cover with water. Bring slowly to the boil, then reduce the heat and simmer for 1½–2 hours. Turn off the heat and cool slightly.

Remove the ham hock from the stock and shred the meat from the bone. Strain and reserve the stock.

To make the soup, place a saucepan over a medium heat, then add the butter, peas and parsley, 750ml of the hot ham stock and the cream and bring to a simmer. Pour into a blender, making sure to fill it only one-third full, cover with the lid and blitz to a purée. (You will probably have to blend the soup in batches.) You'll know your blender better than I do, but you need to make sure the centre part of the lid is slightly ajar, or it can create a vacuum which can pop the lid off and spray hot soup around the kitchen. Be careful.

Return the soup to the saucepan to heat through, then season with salt and pepper.

Heat a griddle pan until hot, drizzle half the rapeseed oil over the cut side of the bread, then place on the griddle cut-side down and cook until charred, then scrape with the cut side of the garlic cloves.

Ladle the soup into a bowl, top with some of the shredded ham, a drizzle of cream and the last of the rapeseed oil.

BRITISH SEASIDE CHOWDER WITH SAFFRON

Whenever I visit the seaside I'm a sucker for cockles and whelks, but the idea of turning them into a chowder is from farther afield. This is such a quick and simple soup when you have the seafood to hand. Use whatever local shellfish you can get your hands on as long as you stick to the same amounts, but this is a good traditional version.

Serves 4

2 tomatoes

300ml white wine

1kg mixed shellfish: cockles, clams, mussels, winkles, soaked in cold water

50g unsalted butter

1 shallot, finely chopped

1 garlic clove, finely chopped

1 fennel bulb, finely chopped

½ leek, white part only, finely chopped

250g potatoes, peeled and cut into 5mm pieces

2 pinches of saffron strands

1 star anise

500ml chicken stock

175ml double cream

75g samphire, trimmed

12 shelled cooked whelks

2 tbsp finely chopped chives

handful of celery leaves

sea salt and freshly ground black pepper

First, skin and deseed the tomatoes: bring a saucepan of water to the boil, take out the stalk of the tomatoes and make crosses on the bases.

Drop the tomatoes into the water and simmer for 10–15 seconds until the skin starts to peel away. Lift straight out into a bowl of iced water and peel off the skin. Cut the tomatoes into quarters and remove the seeds, then finely chop the flesh.

Heat a sauté pan until hot, add the wine and the shellfish, cover and cook for three to five minutes until just cooked through. Strain into a colander over a bowl, reserving the cooking liquor, and allow to cool slightly before picking the meat out of the shells.

Wipe out the sauté pan, then add the butter, shallot and garlic and sweat for a couple of minutes, then add the fennel, leek, potatoes, saffron and star anise and cook for another minute.

Add the reserved cooking liquor and chicken stock and bring to the boil. Reduce the heat to a simmer and cook for three to four minutes until the potatoes are just tender.

Add the cream and samphire then simmer for another couple of minutes until just thickened. Reduce the heat then add the tomatoes and all the shellfish, including the whelks, and gently warm through. Add the chives and celery leaves and season to taste (you probably won't need much salt).

Serve straight away.

PARMA HAM-WRAPPED MOZZARELLA WITH PLUM CHUTNEY

I'm lucky to have mozzarella made just down the road from me. You can now buy it online and in supermarkets and it needs to be as fresh as possible. Buying it in the UK from a UK supplier is a bonus. Plus the farmer is a old F1 world champion… what more encouragement do you need to buy some?

Serves 4

For the plum chutney

75g caster sugar
500g plums, pitted and roughly chopped
1 shallot, finely chopped
50ml malt vinegar
1 star anise
½ tsp ground cinnamon
sea salt and freshly ground black pepper

For the wrapped mozzarella

8 slices of parma ham, halved lengthways
4 balls of buffalo mozzarella, drained and quartered
3 tbsp olive oil
2 tsp sesame seeds
8 slices of ciabatta

For the chutney, heat a frying pan until hot, add the caster sugar and cook without stirring until melted and a light golden brown colour, swirling the pan from time to time. Add the plums, shallot, vinegar, star anise and cinnamon and cook for five to eight minutes until tender and slightly pulpy. Season with a little salt and pepper. Set aside.

Wrap a slice of parma ham around each quarter mozzarella ball to encase the cheese. Ideally, it should cover as much of the cheese as possible.

Heat a large frying pan until hot, add 1 tbsp of the olive oil and fry the parcels on each side until just crispy and the mozzarella is starting to ooze. Sprinkle over the sesame seeds.

Heat a griddle pan until searing hot, then drizzle the rest of the olive oil over the ciabatta and place on to the griddle. Char on each side for one or two minutes until golden brown.

Spoon some chutney on to plates, lay wedges of the mozzarella alongside, then add a couple of slices of bread.

I love rarebit and, when you make a batch of the cheese sauce at home, it can sit in the fridge, covered, for about a week, ready to use on toast or just as it is here. It is even great spooned over cooked smoked fish such as haddock. Use a good cheddar though and don't boil it, or the fat will spill out of the cheese and the mixture will split.

Serves 4

For the apple chutney

150g soft light brown sugar
100g sultanas
125ml malt vinegar
2 eating apples, roughly chopped
3 tomatoes, roughly chopped
1 onion, finely chopped
sea salt and freshly ground black pepper

For the rarebit

8 rashers of dry-cured back bacon
350g grated mature cheddar cheese
50ml beer (I mean ale, not lager)
1 tsp English mustard
3–4 dashes Tabasco sauce
1 tsp Worcestershire sauce
2 tbsp plain flour
4 thick slices of white bread

To sterilise jars for keeping preserves, you have two choices. Either place the jars in a dishwasher on a normal cycle, then fill (taking care not to touch any of the inside of the jar or lid). Or wash the jars in hot soapy water, dry carefully, then place in an oven preheated to 150°C/300°F/gas mark 2 for 15 minutes. Remove carefully and fill immediately.

To make the chutney, heat a sauté pan until hot, add the brown sugar and sultanas and heat until just melting. Don't stir, but swirl the pan from time to time. Add the vinegar and cook until totally dissolved and starting to caramelise, then add the apples, tomatoes and onion and cook for 10 minutes until the apple is tender and the mixture thickened. Season with salt, remove from the heat and decant into a sterilised jar or jars while both chutney and jar are still hot.

For the rarebit, preheat the grill to high. Place the bacon on a tray and grill for four to six minutes, turning once, until the rashers are golden at the edges and just cooked through.

Place the cheese and beer into a frying pan and heat over a low heat until the cheese starts to melt. Heat until bubbling and smooth, then stir in the mustard, Tabasco and Worcestershire sauces, then stir in the flour and cook until just thickened. Season with salt and pepper.

Meanwhile, toast the bread on each side then lay into an ovenproof dish. Top each piece with two rashers of the bacon and spoon the cheese mixture over the top.

Grill for two or three minutes until golden and bubbling. Serve with a dollop of apple chutney.

BASIL TORTELLINI WITH RICOTTA AND PINE NUTS

Adding the basil leaves to the pasta gives it some colour. Try making your own pasta as it's simple, plus you will probably have a pasta machine gathering dust in the cupboard anyway. You can fill the pasta with whatever cheese you wish, but nothing too strong as the basil flavour needs to come through.

Filled tortellini freezes well. Use any leftover pasta to roll out again and make into tagliatelle.

Serves 4 as a starter or light lunch

For the pasta
200g '00' pasta flour, plus more to dust
2 eggs, lightly beaten
12 large basil leaves, plus about
  20 small basil leaves, plus more to serve
225g buffalo ricotta, or cow's milk ricotta
60g toasted pine nuts, to serve
grated parmesan, to serve

For the pesto
50g basil leaves
10g toasted pine nuts
25g parmesan, grated
1 garlic clove, bashed
25ml extra virgin olive oil
50ml olive oil
sea salt and freshly ground black pepper

Place the flour and eggs into a food processor and pulse until the mixture forms small crumbs. Tip it out on to a work surface and squish into a ball, then knead for a few minutes until smooth. Wrap in cling film and chill for 20 minutes in the fridge.

Meanwhile, make the pesto. Place the basil, pine nuts, parmesan and garlic into a mortar and pestle and bash until deep green and broken down, then gradually add both the oils, pounding all the time. Season with salt and freshly ground black pepper.

Lightly flour the business end of a pasta machine. Cut the pasta into three and flatten out about 1cm thick. Starting at the lowest (thickest) setting, feed a piece of dough through the machine, turning the handle with one hand and holding the dough as it comes through with the other.

Change the setting on the pasta machine to the next-thickest setting, flour it again and feed the pasta sheet through the machine again, as before.

Repeat this process three or four more times, flouring the machine and changing the setting down each time, until the last-but-one setting. It helps to cut the pasta into smaller pieces during this process, as this will mean it is less likely to dry out; you should end up with about six sheets. (Any pasta you are not working on should be covered with cling film.) Take one long sheet and place two of the large basil leaves on to the bottom half of it, then fold the other half over to cover and pass back through the pasta machine on its finest setting; you should get two elongated basil leaves running through it. Repeat with the remaining pasta and large basil leaves.

Cut the pasta into 9cm discs with a pasta cutter or cookie cutter.

Place a small spoonful of ricotta on to a small basil leaf, then place this in the centre of each disc. Brush around the edges with a little water. Fold the top over to seal the basil-wrapped ricotta inside. Twist each corner towards the centre to meet and form a ring and press together, then set aside. You need five pieces per portion and you should make 20 pieces from this mixture.

Bring a large pan of salted water to the boil, drop the tortellini in and cook for three or four minutes or until they float to the surface, drain and return to the pan. Add the pesto and toss to coat and finish cooking the pasta through, then toss in the pine nuts to serve.

Serve immediately with a generous grating of parmesan and a few small basil leaves.

ASPARAGUS, CURED HAM, POACHED DUCK EGG AND HOLLANDAISE

I love duck's eggs. They are larger than hen's eggs, so need a few more minutes to cook. Hollandaise is a simple sauce that can go wrong very easily, but it needn't with just a few rules: melt the butter, cool it, then add it to the eggs slowly.

Serves 4 as a starter or light lunch

For the asparagus, ham and eggs
sea salt and freshly ground black pepper
2 tbsp white wine vinegar
4 duck's eggs
16 asparagus stalks, stems peeled and trimmed
a little olive oil
8 slices air-cured ham, ideally British,
   or serrano or parma

For the hollandaise
125g unsalted butter
50ml white wine vinegar
1 shallot, finely chopped
½ tsp black peppercorns
2 large free-range (hen's) egg yolks

First, poach the eggs. Bring a wide pan of salted water to the boil and add the vinegar. Crack one egg into a small bowl. Whisk the water to create a whirlpool then carefully drop the egg into the vortex. Simmer for three to four minutes, then carefully lift the egg out and place into a bowl of iced water. Repeat with the remaining eggs. Set aside the pan and its water.

For the hollandaise, place the butter in a hot saucepan, then turn the heat off and set aside. Place the vinegar, shallot and peppercorns into a separate small pan and heat until just boiling, then simmer until reduced by half.

Place the egg yolks into a food processor with a pinch of salt and turn on. With the motor running, slowly add the melted butter – drip by drip at first – until it is all incorporated. Pour into a bowl, strain in the reduced vinegar (discarding the shallot and peppercorns), season to taste, then cover and keep warm in a bowl set over a pan of hot water.

Working quickly, return the wide pan of salted water to the boil, add the asparagus and simmer for three to four minutes, depending on the thickness of the asparagus, until tender when pierced with a knife. Lift out of the water and drain on kitchen paper.

Return the eggs and heat for 20–30 seconds, then drain on kitchen paper.

Divide the asparagus between four plates, top each with an egg and slivers of the ham, then spoon over some warm hollandaise. Sprinkle everything with salt and pepper and serve.

CONFIT DUCK SALAD WITH BLUE CHEESE DRESSING

The great chef Eric Chavot gave me this dressing and I use it all the time; the buttermilk gives it the acidity you need. Duck confit can be found in most supermarkets now in cans, so you can make this dish nice and quickly. I hope you like it; I think it's one of the best salads out there. Whenever I'm doing dinners at mine, this recipe is a must.

Serves 2 – 4

2 confit duck legs
75g soft light brown sugar
pinch of cayenne pepper
100g pecan nuts
sea salt and freshly ground black pepper
75g gorgonzola, roughly chopped
50g St Agur blue cheese, roughly chopped
1 garlic clove, finely chopped
2 tbsp runny honey
50ml buttermilk
60g crème fraîche
juice of 1 lemon
dash of Tabasco
2 dashes of Worcestershire sauce
1 tbsp red wine vinegar
75g mayonnaise
1 head Romaine lettuce, cut into
* 2.5cm-thick slices*

Preheat the oven to 200°C/400°F/gas mark 6. Put the duck legs on to a tray and place in the oven for 10 minutes to heat through.

Meanwhile, heat a frying pan until hot, add the sugar and cayenne pepper then, when the sugar stars to melt, add 50ml of water and swirl to combine.

Cook over a high heat until a deep caramel, then add the pecan nuts and stir to coat. Add a pinch of salt. Tip out on to a baking tray and place in the oven for five minutes while you make the dressing.

Put both cheeses into a bowl and whisk to break down the cheese slightly, then add the garlic, honey, buttermilk and crème fraîche and whisk together well.

Add the lemon juice, Tabasco, Worcestershire sauce, vinegar and mayonnaise and whisk well, then season with salt and pepper.

Remove the duck and pecans from the oven and wait until they're cool enough to handle, then shred the duck from the bone.

Toss the lettuce with some of the cheese dressing – just enough to coat the leaves – then add the shredded duck and pecans and toss together.

Pile into a large bowl, drizzle with more of the dressing and serve straight away, with the remaining dressing in a bowl alongside.

SMOKED SALMON, PRAWN AND CUCUMBER MOUSSE

As I was making this, the team started laughing at me. They didn't when they tasted it. It looks so impressive and, frankly, so 70s, but so what? My mum used to do something like this. Actually she used to buy it, hide the packaging and fob it off as home-made. Well mother, the shop you used to use is shut. This is the real recipe and it's so easy.

Serves 6

a little rapeseed oil
1 large cucumber, peeled and very finely sliced
400g unsliced smoked salmon, chopped
*juice of 1 lemon, or to taste, plus lemon wedges
    to serve*
200g full-fat cream cheese
450ml double cream
sea salt and freshly ground black pepper
300g cooked prawns, shelled and deveined
50g watercress
6 cooked tiger prawns in the shell
melba toast, to serve

Use a little rapeseed oil to oil a shallow 22cm diameter, 4.5cm deep savarin mould, then line with cling film, making sure it overlaps the mould all the way around.

Layer most of the cucumber into the mould, overlapping the slices as if they were fish scales, so that they cover all of the inside of the mould. Set aside.

Put the chopped smoked salmon into a food processor with the lemon juice and blitz until smooth. Add the cream cheese and blitz once more, then, with the food processor running, slowly add the double cream until the mixture is thickened and smooth, scraping the mixture down halfway through. Season with salt and pepper and adjust the lemon juice to taste.

Carefully spoon the mixture into a piping bag, then pipe half the mixture into the base of the cucumber-lined mould. Top with half the prawns, then cover with the remaining mousse.

Smooth it flat with a palette knife and cover the top with the remaining cucumber. Pull the cling film up to cover, then place in the fridge for 30 minutes or until ready to serve.

Peel back the cling film, then place the mould upside down on a serving plate. Gently lift off the mould and peel back the cling film.

Pile the watercress and remaining prawns in a pile in the centre of the mould. Decorate with the tiger prawns. Serve with wedges of lemon and plenty of melba toast.

CRISPY CHEESE NUGGETS WITH GRAPE CHUTNEY AND PECAN SALAD

The team named these nuggets, but there isn't a fancier name really. Think of them as nuggets of gold, though, rather than the other famous fried nuggets… The chutney works so well with them, but bought stuff could be used, too.

Serves 4–6

For the chutney

100g light muscovado sugar
1 onion, finely chopped
100g sultanas
150ml sherry vinegar
2 tomatoes, roughly chopped
300g red grapes, halved
sea salt and freshly ground black pepper

For the pecan salad

100g caster sugar
100g pecan halves
2 heads little gem lettuce, leaves separated
2 tbsp 'house' dressing (see page 75)

For the cheese nuggets

flavourless vegetable oil, to deep-fry
125g plain flour
4 eggs, lightly beaten
150g fresh breadcrumbs
400g assorted cheese, cut into 3cm chunks

Heat a large frying pan until hot, add the muscovado sugar and heat until the sugar is just caramelising. Don't stir, but swirl the pan from time to time. Add the onion and sultanas then pour in the sherry vinegar. Add the tomatoes and grapes and cook for 12–15 minutes, or until the grapes are tender and the mixture has thickened. Season with salt and pot into a sterilised jar (see page 21).

For the salad, pour 100ml of water into a saucepan and add the sugar. Bring to a boil and simmer until the sugar has dissolved and the syrup thickened slightly. Add the pecans and cook for two or three minutes, then transfer to a plate lined with greaseproof paper.

Heat a deep-fat fryer to 180°C/350°F or heat the oil for deep-frying in a deep heavy-based saucepan until a breadcrumb sizzles and turns brown when dropped in. (CAUTION: hot oil can be dangerous. Do not leave unattended.)

Carefully place the pecans, a few at a time, into the hot oil for a couple of minutes, or until golden-brown. Remove using a slotted spoon and transfer to a plate lined with greaseproof paper. Set aside to cool.

To make the cheese nuggets, tip the flour into a shallow bowl and put the egg and breadcrumbs into another two shallow bowls. Pass the chunks of cheese through the flour, turning to coat on all sides, then through the beaten egg. Finally roll each through the breadcrumbs to coat.

Carefully lower a batch into the hot fat and fry for 30–60 seconds until golden, softened and hot through. Drain on kitchen paper and keep warm while you cook the rest

Place the little gem leaves in a bowl, drizzle the dressing over, then scatter in the cooled pecans and toss to coat.

Top with the crispy cheese nuggets and finish with a spoonful of chutney.

FRUITS DE MER WITH HOME-MADE RYE BREAD AND WHIPPED BUTTER

What a treat; fresh seafood is one of the joys of being alive. I have this whenever I can. Home-made rye bread is what I love to eat it with it and whipping the butter makes it light. Mayonnaise is all you need alongside. This is all about the best-quality shellfish and, around the UK, we have some of the best in the world.

Serves 4

For the rye bread and butter

500g whole grain rye flour, plus more to dust
25g dark brown muscovado sugar
10g salt
10g fast-action dried yeast
350ml water
200g unsalted butter, softened

For the fruits de mer

12 langoustines
12 razor clams, scrubbed
400g clams in the shell, scrubbed
1 x 1kg cooked lobster
1 cooked medium brown crab
8 oysters, shucked
16 cooked shrimps in the shell
200g cooked brown shrimps

For the mayonnaise

3 egg yolks
1 tbsp Dijon mustard
2 tbsp cider vinegar
finely grated zest and juice of 1 unwaxed lemon
300ml rapeseed oil
sea salt and freshly ground black pepper

Start the rye bread the day before. Place the flour, sugar and salt into a large bowl or a food mixer fitted with a dough hook. Put the yeast into a jug with 200ml of the water and mix to combine, then turn on the mixer and slowly add the yeasted water, then measure in the rest of the water to the jug and add gradually to the dough, making sure you've pulled all the flour from the bottom into the dough.

Tip out on to a very lightly floured work surface, then knead well for at least five to 10 minutes until elastic.

Form into a long log shape, then set on to a baking parchment-lined baking sheet, cover loosely with cling film to allow for the dough to double in size, but make a good seal around the edges to keep it as airtight as possible. Set aside to prove for at least six hours, but preferably overnight.

Preheat the oven to 220°C/425°F/gas mark 7. Uncover the dough and dust with a little rye flour, then slash the top diagonally a few times with a sharp knife. Place the loaf into the oven and bake for 30 minutes. When the bread is risen and golden brown, tap the base of the loaf: it should sound hollow when it is ready. Allow to cool.

Place the softened butter into a food processor and blitz until light and fluffy, then scrape into a serving dish.

Place the langoustines into a steamer insert set on a saucepan half filled with water, then place the razor clams and clams into a second level of steamer on top. Cover with a lid and steam for five to eight minutes until they are all cooked through. Set aside.

Prepare the lobster by cutting it in half lengthways, remove any gubbins in the head and remove the claws. Break down into knuckles and claws, then tap firmly with the back of a heavy knife to crack them. Pick the meat out of both and pile back into the shell.

Prepare the crab by opening the shell, remove the dead man's fingers and discard. Remove the claws and repeat as for the lobster, then pile back into the crab shell.

For the mayonnaise, whisk the egg yolks, mustard, vinegar and lemon juice in a bowl or small processor. Still whisking, start adding the rapeseed oil in a very thin trickle; the mixture should be thick and light once the oil is incorporated. Stir in the lemon zest and season to taste, then decant into a serving bowl.

Pile the seafood on to a big platter and serve with the lemon mayonnaise, sliced rye bread and whipped butter.

VANILLA-CURED SALMON WITH CUCUMBER KETCHUP, CHARRED CUCUMBER AND HOME-PICKLED GINGER

It's so easy to make cured salmon: all it needs is salt, sugar and a bit of time in the fridge. The ketchup doesn't need any cooking. It uses xantham gum (buy that from health food shops) which thickens the mixture while in the blender.

Serves 8–10

For the salmon

2 whole vanilla pods, roughly chopped
200g caster sugar
200g sea salt
1.5g salmon fillet, skin on, pin-boned, rinsed
    and patted dry
bunch of breakfast radishes, halved lengthways
punnet of mustard cress

For the cucumber (ketchup and charred)

2 cucumbers
100ml rice wine vinegar
1 tsp caster sugar
1 tsp sea salt
2–3 tsp xantham gum
a little rapeseed oil

For the pickled ginger

100ml rice wine vinegar
pinch of caster sugar
pinch of sea salt
5cm root ginger, peeled and finely julienned

Start with the salmon. Put the vanilla and sugar in a food processor and blitz to a fine purée, then stir in the salt.

Place four pieces of cling film, slightly overlapping, on a clean work surface, then put half the sugar mixture in a line down the centre.

Place the salmon fillet on top, skin-side down, then sprinkle the rest of the mixture over the top to cover the salmon. Wrap the salmon up loosely in the cling film, then place it on a tray in the fridge for 24 hours.

Remove the salmon from the cling film, brush off the salt mixture and rinse the fish thoroughly under cold water, then pat dry and wrap in cling film until ready to serve.

For the cucumber ketchup, trim the outer edges of the cucumbers off so that you are left with two long 2cm square rectangles. Set those aside. Roughly chop the trimmings of the cucumber, then put into a food processor with the rice wine vinegar, sugar and salt. Blitz to a fine purée, then add the xanthan gum 1 tsp at a time until it thickens.

For the charred cucumber, chop the long rectangles of cucumber into batons, discarding the central seedy bits. Heat a griddle pan until hot, drizzle the batons with a little rapeseed oil, then cook on each side until charred and hot through. Remove from the heat and cut into small cubes.

To make the pickled ginger, place the vinegar, sugar and salt into a medium saucepan and heat until the sugar has dissolved. Add the ginger and simmer for one or two minutes until the ginger has wilted down. Remove from the heat and leave to cool.

Slice the salmon finely as you would smoked salmon: take a long sharp knife and cut thin slices on the diagonal, cutting the fish away from the skin. Lay on plates, top with pieces of the charred cucumber, blobs of the cucumber ketchup and the halved radishes. Scatter the pickled ginger and mustard cress over the top to finish.

Quick food shouldn't mean food lacking in taste, so there are some great techniques and tips in this chapter to improve a quick supper or lunch. Some may call using ready-made food such as chips cheating, but I call it a good idea. Anything that helps save time must be a good thing.

Quick comforts

DOUBLE-BAKED OLD WINCHESTER SOUFFLÉ WITH DANDELION AND WALNUT SALAD

These soufflés freeze really well and can be cooked from frozen with the sauce and the cheese on top (give them an extra five minutes in the oven).

Together with the salad, these fluffy delights make a full meal. I came across Old Winchester cheese while making the TV show; it proves you can always make delicious discoveries on your own doorstep.

Serves 4 as a starter or light lunch

For the soufflés

40g softened unsalted butter, plus more for the ramekins
40g plain flour, plus more to dust
350ml whole milk
125g Old Winchester or other mature hard cheese, grated
1 tsp Dijon mustard
3 eggs, separated
sea salt and freshly ground black pepper

For the salad

110g caster sugar
110g walnut halves
flavourless vegetable oil, to deep-fry
110g dandelion leaves
chopped chives, to serve
3 tbsp 'house' dressing (see page 75)

For the glaze

250ml double cream
4 tbsp kirsch
100g Old Winchester or other mature hard cheese, grated

To make the soufflés, preheat the oven to 180°C/350°F/gas mark 4. Rub the inside of four 150ml ramekins with the softened butter, then dust with flour and place in a high-sided oven tray.

Melt the butter in a large saucepan over a medium heat, then add the flour and mix well. Cook over a low heat for two or three minutes, stirring with a wooden spoon. Gradually whisk in the milk, a little at a time, stirring constantly to avoid any lumps forming. Continue until all the milk has been added, then reduce the heat to very low and cook for a further two or three minutes.

Add the cheese and mustard, then take off the heat and beat the egg yolks into the mixture. Season with salt and black pepper.

In a clean, dry bowl, whisk the egg whites until they hold medium peaks, then fold the egg whites into the soufflé mixture. Divide the mixture between the soufflé dishes and put the ramekins in a roasting tin.

Pour enough hot water from the kettle into the tin to reach halfway up the sides of the ramekins. Bake the soufflés for 15–20 minutes, or until they are risen and evenly coloured.

Remove the ramekins from the tin and set aside for a few minutes, then run a knife around the edges of the soufflés and turn them out on to individual ovenproof dishes.

Make the salad. Pour 110ml of water into a saucepan, add the sugar and bring to the boil. Simmer until the sugar has dissolved and the syrup has thickened slightly. Add the walnuts and cook for two or three minutes. Empty the pan on to a sheet of baking parchment placed on a baking sheet.

Pour enough vegetable oil into a sauté pan to cover the bottom by 2cm and heat until just shimmering. Carefully place the walnuts a few at a time into the hot oil for a couple of minutes until golden brown. Drain on a sheet of baking parchment and leave to cool.

For the glaze, preheat the grill to medium-high. Whisk the cream and kirsch until combined. Coat the tops of the soufflés with the cream, then scatter over the cheese and place under the grill until golden. Serve in their dishes, or transfer to plates.

Put the dandelion leaves and chives into a bowl and toss in the dressing and nuts. Pile the salad on top of the soufflé and serve immediately.

CLASSIC PRAWN COCKTAIL WITH LANGOUSTINES

The 1970s are back… well, they should be, as people seem to love stuff like this when I have dinners at home. If you like you could push the boat out and make melba toast but, for heaven's sake, stop at a melon boat. There is only so much us 70s children can cope with.

Serves 4 as a starter

600g raw tiger prawns, shell on
600g raw langoustines, shell on
2 egg yolks
1 tsp Dijon mustard
300ml vegetable oil
1 tsp Worcestershire sauce
4 dashes of Tabasco sauce
25ml brandy
50ml tomato ketchup
sea salt and freshly ground black pepper
2 lemons
3 Little Gems, leaves separated
2 tbsp 'house' dressing (see page 75)
2 tbsp mustard cress
½ tsp cayenne pepper
buttered brown bread, to serve

Place the prawns into a steamer set over a pan of boiling water. Cover and cook for 2½ minutes, then add the langoustines and cook for a further 1½ minutes until the prawns and langoustines turn pink and are just cooked through.

Remove and allow to cool on a plate for 10 minutes before peeling and deveining if necessary.

Meanwhile, place the egg yolks and mustard into a food processor and blend until pale and creamy. With the motor running, pour in enough oil, in a very thin stream, until the mayonnaise is thick. You may not need all the oil.

Place the mayonnaise into a bowl, then add the Worcestershire sauce, Tabasco, brandy and tomato ketchup. Check the seasoning, add a squeeze of lemon juice and mix well. Cut the remaining lemon into four wedges.

Place the Little Gem leaves into a bowl and toss with the dressing, then layer into a cocktail glass.

Lay the peeled langoustines and prawns over the top, then spoon over the sauce and finish with a scattering of mustard cress, a pinch of cayenne pepper and a wedge of lemon. Serve with the buttered brown bread.

BLACK BEAN CHICKEN WITH STIR-FRIED RICE AND WILTED BOK CHOI

This recipe is all about speed, so get things ready and all your prep done and go for it. I know there are a few pans on the go and plenty of food to cook, but it's so quick and easy. Chinese food at its best: fast and tasty. (When preparing cold, cooked rice, make sure you cool the rice down quickly, cover and store in the fridge to minimise the risk of bacterial growth. Never leave it there for more than a day or so.)

Serves 2

2 skinless boneless chicken breasts,
    cut into 1cm-thick slices

3 tbsp light soy sauce

3 tbsp Shaoxing rice wine (or dry sherry)

2 tbsp toasted sesame oil

2 tbsp cornflour

4 tbsp vegetable oil

10cm root ginger, peeled and finely chopped

3 large garlic cloves, finely chopped

3 red chillies, finely chopped

50g fermented black beans

1 tbsp caster sugar

150ml chicken stock

6 spring onions, finely sliced

4 tbsp roughly chopped coriander leaves

2 heads of bok choi, halved or quartered,
    depending on size

200g basmati rice, cooked, drained and chilled

1 egg

Put the chicken in a bowl with 1 tbsp each of the soy sauce, Shaoxing or sherry and sesame oil. Add all the cornflour, then mix to combine. Leave to marinate for 10 minutes.

Heat a wok or large frying pan over high heat until it is hot. Add 1 tbsp of the vegetable oil and, when it is hot and slightly smoking, add the chicken. Stir-fry for two or three minutes until nearly cooked through. Lift out with a slotted spoon and set aside, then wipe out the wok and return to the heat.

Add another 1 tbsp of the vegetable oil and, when it's hot and slightly smoking again, add one-third of each of the ginger, garlic and chillies and all the black beans and stir-fry for two to three minutes until just softened. Add the remaining Shaoxing, 1 tbsp of the soy, the sugar and stock and bring to the boil, then return the chicken and cook for one or two minutes until the sauce has thickened slightly and the chicken cooked through.

Finish by stirring in one-third of the spring onions and coriander.

Set aside and heat another wok until hot, add another 1 tbsp of vegetable oil, half of each of the remaining ginger, garlic and chillies and stir-fry for one minute, then add the bok choi and 75ml of water and steam/stir-fry until the bok choi is tender and the liquid has evaporated. Add half the remaining coriander and spring onions and stir-fry for one minute.

Wipe out the wok and return to the heat, then add the last of the vegetable oil, ginger, garlic and chillies and stir-fry for one minute, then add the rice and stir-fry for another minute.

Crack the egg into the centre of the wok, then stir-fry for a couple more minutes so the rice is hot and the egg cooked through.

Stir in the last of the sesame oil, coriander and spring onions and fry for a final minute.

Pile the rice on to plates, spoon some chicken next to it, then finish with the bok choi.

A 'French-trimmed' chicken breast is a skin-on breast with the wing bone attached, but the end of the bone is trimmed down like a French-trimmed rack of lamb. You're best off asking your butcher to cut them for you. And most people wouldn't think you can cook squash in super-quick time… but you can and it's so easy.

Serves 2

1 butternut or tromboncino squash
2 French-trimmed skin-on chicken breasts
    (wing bones attached)
sea salt and freshly ground black pepper
50g unsalted butter
1 tbsp olive oil
1 shallot, finely chopped
2 garlic cloves, finely sliced
1 tbsp caster sugar
5cm root ginger, finely grated
½ tsp turmeric
¼ tsp fenugreek seeds
1½ tsp black onion seeds
1 red chilli, deseeded and finely chopped
2 tbsp roughly chopped coriander leaves
2 tbsp mango chutney

Preheat the oven to 200°C/400°F/gas mark 6. Cut a 6cm piece of squash and peel it, then cut into four 1.5cm-thick slices and set aside.

Cut another piece of squash about 300g in weight, peel it and chop into 1cm pieces.

Season the chicken breasts with salt and pepper.

Heat an ovenproof frying pan until hot, making sure it is large enough to hold the chicken and squash slices in a single layer. Add half the butter, the olive oil and the chicken, skin-side down. Cook on each side for one to two minutes until golden brown. Now add the squash slices, turn to coat and place in the oven for 15 minutes, until both are cooked through. The squash should be tender to the point of a knife, and the chicken, when cut at its thickest point, should show no trace of pink. (If it does, return to the oven for a few minutes, then test again.)

Meanwhile, heat a sauté pan until hot, add the remaining butter and the shallot, garlic and chopped squash and cook for a couple of minutes.

Add the sugar and cook until just caramelising, then add a splash of water with the ginger, turmeric, fenugreek and black onion seeds and cook for another couple of minutes.

Pour in 50–75ml of water and stir to combine, then add the chilli, coriander and a good pinch of salt and cook for a further two minutes. Remove from the heat and stir in the mango chutney.

Place two slices of squash on to each plate, top with a chicken breast, then spoon some spiced squash alongside.

TERIYAKI MUSHROOM RISOTTO WITH RED MULLET AND LIME LEAF FOAM

This dish has travelled a fair bit, it came from when I was in the southern Indian ocean cooking with a Spanish chef. He had worked in some amazing places and this is an idea he had. It's cheffy, I know, but not that hard. The main thing is the quality of the mushrooms. Red mullet works with it, but you can serve it with any fish, or without. A common mistake people make with risotto is to make it too thick and heavy; keep it loose and add more stock if needed. You've been told…

Serves 4

250g mixed oyster and shiitake mushrooms
600ml chicken stock, plus more if needed
25g unsalted butter
2 shallots, finely chopped
2 garlic cloves, finely chopped
100g risotto rice
100ml white wine
sea salt and freshly ground black pepper
2 tbsp olive oil
4 tbsp teriyaki sauce
2 tbsp mascarpone
2 tbsp grated parmesan
200ml whole milk
4 kaffir lime leaves, very finely chopped
1 tsp lecithin
4 x red mullet fillets

Prepare the mushrooms, brushing off any dirt, then trimming off the stems and tearing any large ones in half. Pour the stock into a saucepan with the trimmings and stalks from the mushrooms and warm through.

Heat a sauté pan until medium hot, add a knob of the butter, the shallots and garlic and cook for a couple of minutes without colouring, then add the rice and stir well. Pour in the wine and cook until it has disappeared.

Strain the stock into a clean saucepan, discarding any grit at the bottom, and place over a gentle heat. Add a couple of ladlefuls of stock at a time, simmering and stirring until the rice has absorbed all the stock, then add some more and continue to cook. Repeat until all the stock has been used and the rice is tender; it should take 15–18 minutes. Season well.

Heat a non-stick frying pan until hot, add the remaining butter and 1 tbsp of the olive oil, then tip in the mushrooms and cook over a high heat until just golden and tender. Any moisture they release into the pan should have evaporated.

Toss straight into the risotto, then fold in the teriyaki sauce, mascarpone and parmesan. At this point adjust the texture of the risotto if needed. It shouldn't be too thick or heavy, so add a bit more stock to loosen the texture, if necessary.

Pour the milk into a saucepan with the lime leaves and lecithin and bring just to a simmer. Blitz with a stick blender to create a foam.

Put a frying pan on a high heat, add the remaining 1 tbsp of olive oil, then the red mullet, skin-side down. Cook for one minute, then turn and cook for another 30 seconds on the flesh side.

Spoon the risotto into bowls, top with the fish, skin side up, and finish with a spoonful of lime leaf foam.

CAULIFLOWER 'COUSCOUS' WITH BARBECUED CHICKEN AND HONEYED TOMATOES

I love this salad. Henry Dimbleby showed me the idea, but I've done it slightly differently. It's like couscous… but tastier. I love the dressing with the maple syrup and vinegar mixed together. You could just roast the chicken in the oven if you wish rather than barbecue; either way this is all about the great salad that goes with it. Remember to season the cauliflower well.

Serves 4

2 tbsp olive oil

4 chicken breasts, cut in half

sea salt and freshly ground black pepper

8 sprigs of thyme

4 ripe tomatoes, halved widthways

3 tbsp runny honey

1 large cauliflower, cored and broken into florets

250ml maple syrup

6 tbsp white wine vinegar

1 heaped tsp curry powder

75g shelled pistachio nuts, roughly chopped

75g toasted flaked almonds

4 spring onions, sliced

3 tbsp chopped mint leaves

3 tbsp chopped coriander leaves

Prepare a barbecue until the flames have died down and the coals are just glowing. Drizzle half the oil over the chicken breasts and season with salt and pepper, then add half the thyme and toss to coat. Place the chicken skin side down on the barbecue and cook for eight to 10 minutes on each side until golden brown and cooked through.

Place the tomatoes on a sheet of foil cut sides down, fold the foil up around the sides to make a little 'tray', then drizzle with the last of the oil, add the honey, scatter the remaining thyme on top and season with salt and pepper. Place on the barbecue alongside the chicken and roast for 12–15 minutes.

Meanwhile, blitz the cauliflower in a food processor to tiny pieces, then tip into a large bowl. Heat a frying pan until hot, add the maple syrup, vinegar and curry powder and cook for one to two minutes until hot through.

Tip into the bowl with cauliflower, add the pistachios, flaked almonds, spring onions and herbs and stir well, then season to taste with salt and pepper.

Pile the cauliflower 'couscous' into a serving bowl, top with the chicken and tomatoes and drizzle the juices from the tomatoes over the top.

SOURDOUGH COD CHEEKS WITH SPICY PEA SALSA

Cod cheeks are solid lumps of meat with a membrane running through them, which needs to be removed. Cheeks mainly come from cod and monkfish and you can easily find them in good fishmongers or – frozen – online, but, if you can't get hold of them, fish fillets will do. It's easy to find cod cheeks in France; even village markets will sell them.

Serves 4

150g stale sourdough bread, chopped

finely grated zest of 1 unwaxed lemon, plus lemon wedges to serve

75g plain flour

3 eggs, lightly beaten

sea salt and freshly ground black pepper

20 cod cheeks, cleaned, membranes removed

300g frozen peas, defrosted

3 tbsp roughly chopped mint leaves

2 green chillies, deseeded and roughly chopped

juice of 2 limes

100g crème fraîche

flavourless vegetable oil and 100g beef dripping, to deep-fry

Put the bread into a food processor and blitz until crumbs are formed, then add the lemon zest and blitz once more. Tip the lemon crumbs into a shallow bowl and put the flour and egg into another two shallow bowls. Season the flour, then dip the cod cheeks into the flour to coat, then into the egg and finally into the lemon crumbs until totally covered. Cover and set aside in the fridge until ready to serve (you can make these a day in advance).

Wash the food processor out, then make the salsa. Put in the peas, mint, chillies, lime juice and crème fraîche and blitz until chunky; you don't want it to be smooth. Tip out into a serving bowl; this can also be made a day ahead and kept, covered, in the fridge.

Heat a deep-fat fryer to 190°C/375°F, or heat the oil for deep-frying in a deep heavy-based saucepan, until a breadcrumb sizzles and turns brown when dropped into it. (CAUTION: hot oil can be dangerous. Do not leave unattended.)

Drop the cod cheeks into the hot fat in batches, and cook for two or three minutes until golden and cooked through. Drain on kitchen paper while you quickly cook the rest.

Pile the cod cheeks on to a serving plate and serve with lemon wedges and the pea salsa.

COURGETTE AND LEMON ARANCINI WITH DEEP-FRIED COURGETTE FLOWERS

Feed some of the risotto to the kids, then use the cold rice to make arancini later in the evening for the adults. The whole idea is that you only have to cook once to create two meals. It's not leftovers, it's two dishes in one.

Make sure there is plenty of cheese in this as it will melt when cooked. Try stuffing mozzarella inside the arancini, too, before coating and frying.

Serves 4 (2 kids and 2 adults)

For the risotto

750ml chicken stock
25g unsalted butter
2 shallots, finely chopped
1 garlic clove, finely chopped
leaves from 3 sprigs of thyme
200g risotto rice
200ml white wine
200g courgettes, cut into 1cm cubes
4 heaped tbsp grated parmesan, plus more
  to serve
finely grated zest of 1 unwaxed lemon, plus
  1 tbsp lemon juice
sea salt and freshly ground black pepper

For the arancini and deep-fried courgette flowers

flavourless vegetable oil, to deep-fry
50g serrano or parma ham, chopped
4 tbsp grated parmesan
90g plain flour
2 eggs, lightly beaten
75g fresh breadcrumbs
50g cornflour
125ml sparkling water
8 courgette flowers
1 lemon, cut into wedges

For the risotto, pour the stock into a saucepan and set it over a medium-low heat. Heat a sauté pan until medium hot, add a knob of the butter, the shallots, garlic and thyme and cook for a couple of minutes without colour. Tip in the rice and stir well, then pour in the wine and cook until it has reduced to nothing.

Add a couple of ladlefuls of hot stock at a time, simmering and stirring until the rice has absorbed all the stock, then add more. After seven or eight minutes, add the courgettes and continue to cook until all the stock has been used and the rice is tender; it should take 15–18 minutes. Add the parmesan, lemon zest and juice and season to taste. Serve one-third of it now as a risotto (it's a great meal for kids), with more parmesan. Put the remaining two-thirds on a tray lined with cling film, cover and leave to cool.

Heat a deep fat fryer to 190°C/375°F or heat the oil for deep-frying in a deep heavy-based sauté pan until a breadcrumb sizzles and turns brown when dropped into it. (CAUTION: hot oil can be dangerous. Do not leave unattended.)

Add the chopped ham and parmesan to the cold risotto and mix well, then form into balls, each about the size of a golf ball. Put 40g of the flour, the egg and breadcrumbs separately into three shallow dishes.

Pass the risotto balls through the flour, turning to coat on all sides, then through the beaten egg and finally through the breadcrumbs to coat totally. Carefully lower a batch into the hot fat and fry for two or three minutes until golden and hot through.

Drain on kitchen paper and set aside while you cook the rest – working quickly – in the same way.

For the courgette flowers, put the cornflour, remaining 50g of plain flour and sparkling water into a bowl and whisk quickly to combine to a smooth batter. Add the courgette flowers and gently mix until coated.

Place them into the fat and fry for one or two minutes until golden-brown, then drain on kitchen paper.

Serve the arancini with the courgette flowers, with lemon wedges alongside.

SPOIL-YOURSELF YORKSHIRE WAGYU FILLET STEAK WITH FRIES AND BÉARNAISE SAUCE

I came across Yorkshire Wagyu when we set up my Manchester restaurant and it's ace. It is grown just like the amazing Japanese beef and we can't get enough of it (but a good fillet steak is fine here). Béarnaise sauce is the best with chips or beef. This is my treat when I'm home alone. Obviously, scale up the recipe to serve more people.

Serves 1

flavourless vegetable oil, to deep-fry

125g unsalted butter

3 tbsp tarragon vinegar

3 tbsp white wine

¼ tsp white peppercorns

½ small banana shallot, finely chopped

3 egg yolks

sea salt and freshly ground black pepper

1 tbsp chopped tarragon leaves

juice of ½ lemon (optional)

1 tbsp olive oil

1 x 200g good fillet steak (I love Yorkshire wagyu for a special occasion)

100g frozen chips

Preheat the oven to 200°C/400°F/gas mark 6.

Heat a deep-fat fryer to 190°C/375°F, or heat the oil for deep-frying in a deep heavy-based frying pan until a breadcrumb sizzles and turns brown when dropped into it. (CAUTION: hot oil can be dangerous. Do not leave unattended.)

Put 100g of the butter into a small saucepan and set over a medium heat to melt fairly gently. Wait until it is liquid and all the impurities have risen to the top in a foam. Skim off all the foam. Leave until just tepid.

Place the vinegar, white wine, peppercorns and shallot into a separate small saucepan and bring to the boil. Simmer until the liquid nearly disappears, leaving only about 1 tbsp.

Put the egg yolks into a bowl, then set over a pan of simmering water and whisk until thickened and light in colour.

Gradually add the melted butter, drop by drop, whisking constantly. Once the mixture has emulsified, add it in a thin stream. You want a sauce that is about the same thickness as mayonnaise. Stop adding the butter just before you get to the white milky solids at the bottom of the pan (discard these). Season the sauce with salt and pepper, add the cooled vinegar reduction and the chopped tarragon leaves and mix well. Taste and see if you want to add lemon juice. Turn off the heat and leave the bowl over the pan until ready to use. Don't leave it too long, and work quickly.

Heat an ovenproof frying pan until searing hot, add the oil and steak then leave to cook on one side for two or three minutes before turning over and placing in the oven for two or three minutes more.

While the steak is in the oven, carefully lower the chips into the fat fryer and cook for three or four minutes until golden brown and cooked through.

Remove the steak from the oven (make sure you wear an oven glove to protect your hands from the frying pan handle) and add the remaining butter to the pan, then spoon over the steak repeatedly for at least two or three minutes while the steak rests; this will give a lovely shine and add to the flavour.

Place the steak on a plate, pile the chips alongside then finish with a dollop of béarnaise.

WHOLE ROAST TROUT WITH SALSA VERDE, ROAST LEMONS AND NEW POTATOES

One of my favourite recipes in the book. I made it up thanks to the great watercress and trout I have around my village. I eat this with spuds from the garden roasted in the wood-fired oven... what more do you want? Fresh trout is so underrated and is one fish we should all be eating more of.

Serves 4
sea salt and freshly ground black pepper
400g new potatoes
1 quantity Salsa verde (see page 13)
1.5kg whole trout, cleaned
3 lemons, halved
herb stalks left over from the salsa verde (mint, dill, tarragon, parsley, watercress and basil)
olive oil

Bring a large pan of salted water to the boil, add the new potatoes and return to the boil. Simmer for 10 minutes, then drain and set aside.

Preheat the oven to 220°C/425°F/gas mark 7.

Make the salsa verde as on page 13.

Put the trout on to a large roasting tray along with the halved lemons and the potatoes. Put a couple of spoonfuls of salsa verde into the cavity of the trout, along with the herb stalks, then drizzle with olive oil and season well with salt and pepper.

Place in the oven and roast for 15–20 minutes until just cooked through.

Serve the trout with the roasted potatoes and lemon halves and a drizzle of salsa verde.

POACHED HADDOCK AND EGG WITH MUSTARD SAUCE

The only dish my grandad was allowed to make and – given my gran was such a great cook – that means a lot. It's simple but it tastes great. You must use proper natural smoked haddock to make it, none of 'that sprayed stuff', as grandad used to call it.

Serves 2

500ml whole milk, plus more if needed
½ onion, thickly sliced
1 bay leaf
2 x 175g natural smoked haddock fillets, pin-boned, skin on
sea salt and freshly ground black pepper
2 tbsp white wine vinegar
2 large eggs
40g unsalted butter
1 tbsp plain flour
1 tbsp English mustard
juice of ½ lemon
200g baby spinach leaves

Preheat the oven to 140°C/275°F/gas mark 1. Pour the milk into a large sauté pan, add the sliced onion and bay leaf and bring to a simmer.

Carefully place the haddock, skin-side down, into the liquid and simmer for two minutes, then turn and simmer for another two minutes.

Meanwhile, bring a small saucepan of water to the boil, add salt and the white wine vinegar, whisk to create a vortex, then crack one egg into the water and cook for three minutes. Remove with a slotted spoon and place straight into iced water, then repeat with the second egg. Keep the pan of water simmering.

Lift the haddock out of the milk with a slotted spoon and place on a plate, then cover and keep the fish warm in the low oven.

Strain the fish poaching milk into a jug, then wipe out the pan and return it to the heat. Add 25g of the butter and, when it has melted, add the flour and cook over a low heat for two or three minutes, stirring with a wooden spoon. Gradually whisk in the reserved milk, a little at a time, whisking constantly to avoid any lumps. Continue until all the milk has been added, then reduce the heat to very low and cook for a further two or three minutes until you have a smooth, shiny sauce.

Add the mustard and check the seasoning and consistency, adding a little more milk if necessary to make it thick enough to coat the back of a spoon. Add lemon juice to taste.

Heat a frying pan until hot, add the remaining butter and the spinach and cook until wilted and hot through. Drain on kitchen paper, then place on serving plates.

Drop the poached eggs back into the pan of simmering water for 20–30 seconds to reheat.

Place a smoked haddock fillet on each pile of spinach, followed by a poached egg, then finish with the mustard sauce over the top.

SIRLOIN STEAK WITH RED WINE AND SNAIL SAUCE

'Snails, you say? Snails?' But in the UK we have snail farmers and on the TV show you might have seen one. Don't go fetching snails from the veg patch, they're not the same thing! And don't diss this recipe until you at least try snails. I was on the snail section once at a restaurant in Paris, so I learned to love them.

Serves 4

1kg floury potatoes, peeled and cut into chunks
sea salt and freshly ground black pepper
225g unsalted butter
150ml double cream
4 x 250g sirloin steaks, at room temperature
1 tbsp olive oil
4 banana shallots, 2 with skin on and cut lengthways in half, 2 peeled and finely chopped
1 garlic clove, finely chopped
25g caster sugar
250ml red wine
175ml veal stock
12 cooked snails, chopped
2 tbsp finely chopped tarragon leaves
2 tbsp chopped flat-leaf parsley leaves

Place the potatoes into a pan of cold, salted water and bring to the boil. Reduce the heat and simmer until the potatoes are tender.

Drain the potatoes and return to the pan, then place over a low heat for a couple of minutes to dry them slightly. Pass the potatoes through a ricer, then add 150g of the butter and the cream and beat to form a very smooth mash, seasoning to taste with salt and pepper. Cover and set aside while you cook the steaks.

Season the steaks with salt. Heat a large frying pan until very hot, add 25g of the butter, the olive oil, steaks and halved shallots, cut sides down. Fry the steaks for three to four minutes on each side, basting with the butter, but leave the shallots cut side down without turning them. Remove everything from the pan and leave to rest on a plate.

Now, working quickly, return the frying pan to the heat, add 25g more of the butter, the chopped shallots and garlic and cook without colour for two or three minutes until softened. Increase the heat to high, add the sugar and, when it's caramelised, add the wine and cook until reduced by half. Add the stock, bring to a simmer and cook for two minutes, then add the snails and heat through.

Whisk in the last 25g of the butter, then season and stir in the herbs.

Lay the steaks on serving plates, take the halved shallots out of their skins and fan the layers over the top of the steak, then spoon the snail sauce over the top. Spoon some mash alongside.

GRANNY'S BACON SARNIE

I know it's just a bacon sandwich… but this is the best I've ever had. Gran used to cook them on one of those old white enamel gas cooker grills with the red knobs. Choose the best bacon and use thick-sliced white bread. Gran bought hers from M&S. She sadly passed away 12 years ago. If I was 10% of what she was, I would be a 100% better person. Granny Smith was a legend, as were her bacon sarnies; she would be proud they are now in print.

Serves 1

4 rashers of dry-cured back bacon
50g salted butter, softened
1 tomato, quartered
2 thick slices of white bread

Put the bacon into a cold frying pan, then increase the heat and cook for a couple of minutes before adding a knob of the butter and the tomato.

Cook, turning once, until the bacon is just golden brown at the edges and cooked through and the tomatoes are softened (five or six minutes).

Slather the bread with the remaining butter and place the tomatoes on to one slice. Press them down slightly, then layer on the bacon and top with the second slice of bread.

Press down lightly to squish it all together, then cut in half and eat, mopping up any spilled butter and juices with the sandwich as you go.

GRUYÈRE AND PANCETTA BRIOCHE SANDWICH

This comes not from France – where brioche is from – but from the States. A baker friend of mine made this for us for breakfast. They have great streaky bacon out there; maple-cured stuff that gets nice and crispy. Here I use pancetta instead. It's a proper hangover cure and – trust me – I needed it that day.

Serves 4

12 rashers of thinly sliced pancetta
2 tbsp maple syrup
8 slices of brioche
4 large slices of gruyère
2 eggs, lightly beaten
1 tsp caster sugar
150ml whole milk
sea salt and freshly ground black pepper
50g unsalted butter

Heat a frying pan until hot, add the pancetta and cook on each side for one or two minutes until just crispy and cooked through. Add the maple syrup, then tip out on to a plate.

Lay four slices of the brioche on a board, top with the gruyère cheese and divide the pancetta and any of its juices between them, then top with the remaining four slices of brioche and press down lightly.

Place the eggs, sugar and milk into a shallow wide bowl, whisk to combine and season with salt and pepper, then dip the sandwiches into the mixture and to soak for a few seconds.

Heat a large frying pan until medium hot, add half the butter and, when it's just foaming, add two of the soaked sandwiches and fry gently on each side until golden and hot through.

Serve straightaway, or keep warm in a low oven if necessary while you cook the remaining sandwiches in the remaining butter.

At first sight, you may not think some of these dishes are easy, but every one is simple prep: maximum impact. These are the recipes I turn to probably more than any others. I hope you like them as much as I do.

Easy comforts

CHICKEN FRICASSEE

Dishes such as this are where I cut my teeth as a chef and learned the true art of great cooking and flavour. This is a classic of French bistro food and it should be cooked at home all the time. Just be careful at the end of the process when adding the yolks to thicken the sauce: watch the pot doesn't boil, or you will have chicken and scrambled eggs. You can use just cream instead, but it works and tastes better with eggs.

Serves 4

For the fricassee

500ml chicken stock
200ml white wine
125g pearl onions
leaves from 3 sprigs of thyme, plus more to serve (optional)
1.5kg whole chicken, cut into 8 pieces, with the rest of its carcass (get a butcher to do this if you prefer)
200g baby button mushrooms
4 egg yolks
150ml double cream
salt and freshly ground black pepper
2 tbsp finely chopped flat-leaf parsley

For the mash

1kg floury potatoes, peeled and cut into chunks
150g unsalted butter
150ml double cream

Place a large casserole over a high heat, add the stock, white wine, onions and thyme and bring to a simmer. Add the chicken, including the carcass, return to a simmer, then tip in the mushrooms. Cover and cook for 15–20 minutes, or until the chicken is cooked through.

Remove the casserole from the heat and lift out the chicken, discarding the carcass. Keep it warm. Let the sauce cool slightly.

Whisk the egg yolks and cream together in a bowl then gradually add to the casserole, whisking constantly as you pour; if the pan is too hot, the eggs will cook too quickly and curdle the sauce.

Return the chicken to the pan, then adjust the seasoning and finally stir in the parsley.

Meanwhile, place the potatoes into a pan of cold, salted water and bring to the boil. Reduce the heat and simmer for 12–15 minutes, or until tender. Make the mash as on page 59.

Spoon the mash into bowls, then top with two pieces of chicken and a ladleful of sauce. Sprinkle with more thyme, if you like.

BEER-MARINATED RACK OF PORK WITH JEFF'S CHARD GRATIN

This to me is a lazy dish: marinate it the day before in a beery brine, then slam it in the oven while watching football on the box. But it tastes great. The idea of the chard gratin came about because I had masses of the stuff I planted in the garden by mistake. Jeff, my gardener, has since taught me that one pack of seeds doesn't make just one row of veg. Thanks Jeff! This dish is now named after you.

Serves 6

For the pork

2 tbsp sea salt

2 tbsp dark brown sugar

1 tsp black peppercorns

4 garlic cloves, lightly crushed

2 bay leaves

2 tbsp yellow mustard seeds, 1 tbsp
    soaked in water overnight

4 sprigs of thyme

4 sprigs of flat-leaf parsley

500ml beer, preferably a good ale

1–1.2kg 6-rib pork loin rack, French-trimmed

50g unsalted butter

100g brioche, roughly torn

1 tsp English mustard powder

1 tbsp brown mustard seeds,
    soaked in water overnight

sea salt and freshly ground black pepper

For the gratin

700g chard, chopped into 2cm pieces

2 large potatoes, peeled and cut into
    1–1.5cm chunks

1 onion, sliced

50g unsalted butter

50g plain flour

400ml whole milk

200ml chicken stock

100g gruyère cheese, grated

Pour 100ml of cold water into a saucepan, add the sea salt and sugar and heat until the sugar dissolves. Remove from the heat. Now mix in 400ml of cold water, the peppercorns, garlic, bay, unsoaked yellow mustard seeds, thyme, parsley and beer.

Put the pork loin into a large bowl or sealable bag then pour in the liquid and cover. Place in the fridge for 24 hours, turning occasionally.

When ready to cook, preheat the oven to 200°C/400°F/gas mark 6. Remove the pork from the bag and pat dry. Heat a large frying pan over a medium heat, then add the butter and heat until foaming. Carefully seal the pork on each side until light golden brown, then transfer to a roasting tray. Roast for 15 minutes.

Put the brioche, mustard powder and soaked yellow and brown mustard seeds into a food processor and blitz to a paste, then season. Set aside.

Meanwhile, make the gratin: layer half the chard and potatoes into an ovenproof dish, scatter over the onion, then place the rest of the chard and potatoes on top.

Put the butter in a saucepan and melt, then add the flour and cook for a couple of minutes until light golden brown. Add the milk gradually, whisking until you have a smooth white sauce, then whisk in the stock and half the cheese and cook until melted. Season with salt and pepper, then pour the sauce over the chard and potatoes and top with the remaining cheese.

After the pork has been cooking for 15 minutes, spread the brioche paste over the top. Decrease the oven temperature to 180°C/350°F/gas mark 4, then return it to the oven for 45 minutes to crisp the crumb and finish cooking the pork through. Place the gratin in the oven at the same time.

Remove the pork from the oven and rest for 15 minutes, while the gratin finishes cooking.

Carve the pork and serve with the chard gratin.

CONFIT DUCK CASSOULET WITH MASH

Duck confit is around in cans in the supermarkets, so it's easy to add to this. Don't be afraid to add some of the duck fat it sits in; that's pure flavour. And calories, of course, but what the hell… If you prefer, you can just cook the first bit of the recipe up to when the sausages and beans have been combined and cooked through; that is a good family meal and kids love it.

Serves 4–5

3 tbsp olive oil

8 good-quality Yorkshire pork sausages

2 shallots, finely chopped

2 garlic cloves, finely chopped

2 tsp roughly chopped rosemary leaves

400g can of tomatoes

400ml chicken stock

400g can of flageolet beans, drained and rinsed

2 tbsp chopped flat-leaf parsley leaves

sea salt and freshly ground black pepper

4–5 thick slices of sourdough bread

50g pancetta lardons

2 confit duck legs, roughly chopped

500g King Edward potatoes, peeled and chopped

50g unsalted butter

75–90ml double cream

Preheat the oven to 200°C/400°F/gas mark 6. Heat a frying pan until hot, add 1 tbsp of the regular oil, then the sausages and cook over a medium heat, turning, until golden brown on each side. Now place in the oven for 10–12 minutes until cooked through.

Meanwhile, heat an ovenproof sauté pan until medium hot, add 1 tbsp more of the regular oil and the shallots and sweat for two minutes, then add the garlic and half the rosemary and sweat for a minute before adding the canned tomatoes. Bring to a simmer, then add 125ml of the stock and the beans and cook for three or four minutes, or until thickened slightly. Add half the parsley and season.

This is a fine meal for kids and you can stop here if you want. To serve, heat a griddle pan until hot, drizzle the last 1 tbsp of the olive oil over two slices of sourdough bread and toast on each side. Place a slice of bread on to two serving plates, divide half the bean mixture between the two, then top each with a sausage and serve.

To make the cassoulet, return the frying pan that was used for the sausages to the heat and, when it's hot, add the pancetta and fry until golden.

Put the remaining cooked sausages into the sauté pan with the remaining bean mixture, then add the lardons and remaining stock and bring to a simmer. Add the remaining rosemary and parsley and the duck and season to taste. Bring to a simmer.

Place the remaining slices of toasted sourdough into a food processor and blitz to fine crumbs. Top the cassoulet with the sourdough crumbs and place into the oven for five to 10 minutes.

Meanwhile, place the potatoes into a pan of salted water and bring to the boil. Reduce the heat and simmer for 12–15 minutes until the potatoes are tender. Drain and return to the pan, then place over the heat for one minute to drive off any excess moisture. Pass through a potato ricer back into the pan, then add the butter and cream, beating to form a smooth mash. Season with salt and pepper.

Serve the cassoulet with some mash.

PENNE CARBONARA

One of my go-to recipes, this is quick and simple but – because it's so pared-down – you must use good-quality ingredients, such as pancetta that will get nice and crisp. Adding the hot drained pasta straight into the sauce cooks the egg yolks, melts the cheese and produces a sauce that coats the pasta really well.

Serves 2 – 4

1 tbsp olive oil
300g thinly sliced pancetta, cut into strips
3 egg yolks
100ml double cream
50g grated parmesan, plus more to serve
3 tbsp roughly chopped flat-leaf parsley leaves
sea salt and freshly ground black pepper
350g fresh or dried penne

Heat a frying pan until hot, add the olive oil and pancetta and cook until crispy; this should take three to five minutes. Drain on kitchen paper, then roughly chop.

Place the egg yolks, cream, parmesan, pancetta and parsley in a bowl and season to taste with salt and pepper.

Bring a pan of salted water to the boil, add the pasta and cook according to the packet instructions. Drain and immediately add the pasta to the cream mixture. Mix well; the heat of the pasta will cook the egg.

Spoon into warmed bowls and grate over some more parmesan.

SALMON AND WATERCRESS PAN BAGNAT

This really is a treat and – to be honest – it's massive! But the idea is you make it and it lasts four to five days in the fridge, or you take it on a picnic and feed the masses. Making the pesto-style sauce with watercress gives a peppery result and uses the masses of watercress for which Hampshire – where I live – is so famous. If you ask me, we should use a lot more of it instead of rocket. It has a great taste and we can grow it naturally all year round.

Serves 8–10

1.5kg salmon fillet
1 lemon, sliced
sea salt and freshly ground black pepper
black peppercorns
leaves from a large bunch of basil
2 garlic cloves
60g toasted pine nuts
400g watercress, coarse stalks removed
400ml extra virgin olive oil
6 courgettes, thinly sliced lengthways
2 tbsp olive oil
1 large good-quality pain de campagne loaf
2 red onions, finely sliced
3 x 200g jars roasted piquillo red peppers, opened out

Preheat the oven to 200°C/400°F/gas mark 6. Place the salmon into a deep-sided tray with the lemon slices, adding salt and black peppercorns. Cover with water, then place in the oven for 15–20 minutes until just cooked through. Remove and allow to cool slightly before flaking the fish into large pieces.

Make the pesto by putting a little salt, the basil, garlic, pine nuts and two-thirds of the watercress into a processor and blitz until slightly chunky, then add the virgin oil gradually until it forms a thick paste.

Heat a griddle pan until very hot. Toss the courgettes with the regular oil, salt and pepper then place on the griddle in batches and cook for one or two minutes until just cooked through. Remove and set aside to cool.

Meanwhile, take the loaf and cut off the top one-quarter. Spread with pesto and set aside. Scoop out all the crumb from inside the loaf and keep for making breadcrumbs. Spread some of the pesto into the bottom of the loaf.

Arrange one-quarter of the onion slices and piquillo peppers over the pesto.

Place one-quarter of the courgettes on top and press down lightly. Place one-quarter of the remaining watercress on top and press down. Top with one-quarter of the salmon. Repeat the layers, including the pesto, until the loaf is full to the brim, then replace the 'lid' on top.

Wrap very tightly in cling film and place in the fridge for at least one hour, but preferably overnight or even up to three days, then unwrap and cut into wedges to serve.

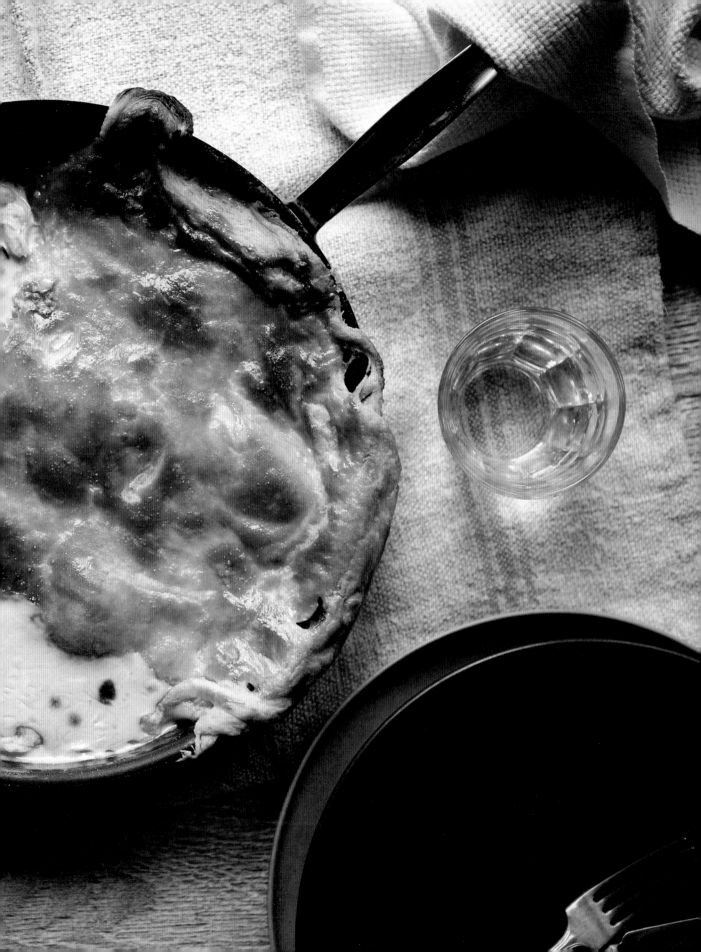

CHICKEN AND WILD MUSHROOM FRYING PAN PIE

Many chefs, when asked how they dreamt up a recipe, will relate a romantic story: perhaps they thought of it while climbing K2 and it was like an epiphany. Truth be told, this dish came about because I'm not one for washing up, I couldn't be bothered to find a dish and I was in a rush. Not K2, I know, but the truth. And it works.

Serves 3 – 4

For the rough puff pastry

250g plain flour, plus more to dust

250g very cold unsalted butter, cut into small cubes

½ tsp salt

For the filling

25g unsalted butter

1 banana shallot, finely chopped

1 garlic clove, finely sliced

2 large skinless boneless chicken breasts, cut into 1cm-thick slices

150g mixed mushrooms, such as chanterelle, girolle and chestnut, sliced if necessary

50ml madeira

150ml chicken stock

2 tbsp chopped tarragon leaves

200ml double cream

sea salt and freshly ground black pepper

2 egg yolks, lightly beaten

For the pastry, place the flour in a mound on a clean work surface and make a well in the centre.

Place the butter and salt in the well and work them together with the fingertips of one hand, gradually drawing the flour into the centre with the other hand. When the cubes of butter have become small pieces and the dough is grainy, gradually add 125ml of ice-cold water and mix until it is all incorporated. But don't overwork the dough; the butter should give a marbled effect to the pastry and not be mixed in fully.

Roll the mixture out on a lightly floured surface into a 2.5cm-thick rectangle, wrap in cling film and refrigerate for 20 minutes.

Flour the work surface and roll out the pastry into a 40 x 20cm rectangle. Fold one short side over by one-third, then the other short side on top of it, as though you were folding a business letter. Turn 90°. Roll the block of pastry into a 40 x 20cm rectangle as before and fold it into three again. These are the first two turns. Repeat twice more to make four turns in total.

Wrap the pastry in cling film and refrigerate for at least 30 minutes before using.

Meanwhile, make the filling. Heat a large (24cm) ovenproof frying pan until hot, add the butter and, when it foams, add the shallot and garlic and fry for one minute, then add the chicken and fry until just coloured. Add the mushrooms and fry over a high heat for two or three minutes until just softened, then add the madeira and set the mixture alight with a match, standing well back.

When the flames subside, pour in the stock and bring to a simmer, then add the tarragon and cream and simmer for five minutes. Check the seasoning, then set aside to cool.

Preheat the oven to 200°C/400°F/gas mark 6.

Roll out the pastry on a lightly floured work surface until it is 5cm wider than the frying pan and 4–5mm thick. Brush the edges of the frying pan with the egg. Lay the pastry over the filling and crimp at the edges. Trim away any excess pastry and brush the top of the pie with the remaining egg. Decorate with any pastry trimmings, if you like.

Bake in the oven for 25 minutes, or until the pastry is crisp and golden and the filling is bubbling.

GRILLED PORK CHOPS WITH ALMOND CROQUETTES AND HOUSE SALAD

When I was growing up on the farm, proper grilled pork chops were what we lived on. That and butter, of course. We never served chops like this – it would be frozen croquettes, if anything – but making your own croquettes makes the potatoes more of a treat and adding the almonds works really well.

Serves 2

150ml vegetable or sunflower oil,
  plus more to deep-fry
2 pork loin chops
1 apple, cored and cut into wedges
sea salt and freshly ground black pepper
1 egg yolk, plus 1 egg, lightly beaten
1 tsp English mustard
2 tsp runny honey
2 tbsp cider vinegar
1 banana shallot, finely chopped
1 garlic clove, finely chopped
2 tbsp finely chopped flat-leaf parsley leaves
1 tbsp finely chopped mint leaves
1 tbsp finely chopped basil leaves
1 tbsp finely chopped thyme leaves
500g mashed potatoes (see page 59)
50g plain flour
75g flaked almonds
1 Little Gem, roughly chopped
2 handfuls lamb's lettuce

Preheat the grill to high and heat the oil for deep-frying in a deep-fat fryer or large saucepan to 180°C/350°F. (CAUTION: hot oil can be dangerous. Never leave the pan unattended.)

Place the pork chops into an ovenproof frying pan along with the apple wedges, then season the pork fat with salt and place under the grill for 10 minutes, turning halfway through.

Meanwhile, make my 'house dressing'. Place the egg yolk into a bowl along with the mustard and honey. Add the cider vinegar and whisk, then gradually add the 150ml of vegetable oil, whisking all the time until thick and creamy.

Add the shallot, garlic, 1 tbsp of the parsley, all the mint, basil and thyme and whisk once more, then check the seasoning and set aside.

Check the seasoning of the mashed potatoes, then add the remaining parsley and mix well. Take a small handful of potato and roll into a sausage shape. Repeat to shape all the mash into croquettes.

Place the flour, beaten whole egg and almonds in three shallow dishes.

Roll the potato sausages in the flour, then the egg and finally in the flaked almonds to coat.

Place into the fryer in batches for two or three minutes until golden, crispy and hot through, then drain on kitchen paper while you cook the rest.

Place the salad leaves in a bowl and add enough dressing to just coat the leaves, then serve alongside the croquettes, pork chops and apples.

SAUSAGE, RADICCHIO AND LEMON GNOCCHI

A great chef mate of mine – Stephen Terry – runs a fab place called the Hardwick at Abergavenny in Wales. If it's a nice day, I often take one of the old cars for a spin and go there for lunch. This was a dish I saw Stephen make and it's so good that I've nicked it both for this book and for me at home. It's very clever cooking from a top-class chef, using just a hint of spice, but the lemon calms it down. Trust me, you will like it.

If you make these ahead, blanch the gnocchi in boiling water as in the recipe, then drain and place on an oiled tray. They will keep better in the fridge and won't turn soft.

Serves 4

For the gnocchi
4 large floury potatoes
olive oil, for the potatoes
4 tbsp rock salt
75g '00' flour, plus more to dust
1 egg yolk
sea salt and freshly ground black pepper
25g parmesan, finely grated

For the sauce
4 good-quality pork sausages, skins removed, roughly chopped
50g unsalted butter
2 shallots, finely chopped
2 garlic cloves, finely chopped
1 tsp chilli flakes, or to taste
300ml chicken stock
100ml double cream
25g capers, rinsed, roughly chopped
2 tbsp roughly chopped flat-leaf parsley leaves, plus more to serve
finely grated zest of 2 unwaxed lemons
1 large head of radicchio, cut into wedges through the root
1 tbsp olive oil
50g fresh white breadcrumbs

For the gnocchi, preheat the oven to 170°C/340°F/gas mark 3½.

Rub the potatoes with a little oil then place on a small pile of rock salt on a baking tray. Bake in the oven for 1½ hours, or until tender. When cooked, remove from the oven and set aside until cool enough to handle.

Cut the potatoes in half and scoop out the flesh, then pass through a potato ricer or sieve into a large bowl. Add the flour and egg yolk, season, then mix lightly until it forms a soft dough.

Tip on to a floured work surface, divide into quarters and roll each into a long sausage. Cut into 2cm pieces and lightly pinch each in the middle.

Once all the gnocchi are cut, drop them into a large pan of boiling salted water. When the gnocchi bob to the surface, they are ready. Remove with a slotted spoon and place in a bowl of ice-cold water to cool.

To make the sauce, heat a frying pan until medium hot, add the sausagemeat and half the butter and fry until golden-brown all over. Add the shallots, garlic and chilli flakes and cook for two minutes.

Pour in the chicken stock and simmer until it is reduced by half and the sausagemeat is cooked through. Add the cream, drained gnocchi, capers, parsley and lemon zest and simmer for two minutes.

Heat a griddle pan until hot, toss the radicchio with the olive oil, then char on the griddle pan for one minute on each side.

Heat a small frying pan until medium hot, add the remaining butter and, when it's foaming, add the breadcrumbs and fry until golden. Season with salt and pepper. Tip the crumbs on to kitchen paper to cool.

Place the radicchio on to a serving plate, then spoon the sauce over the top. Finish with some parmesan and a sprinkling of crunchy breadcrumbs.

CLASSIC CHICKEN KIEV
WITH BEAN RAGOÛT

There are a few dishes in this book which hark back to the 1970s. I'm not so old that I was cooking back then, but my mum's cooking dates back that far. This, together with the rest of the Johnny Mathis collection of recipes in this book, is down to her. It's proper home-cooked grub and for that I thank you, mother: for showing me the way at a young age. Garlic scapes are the stalks and buds of young garlic plants and you can often find them on sale at markets.

Serves 4

175g softened unsalted butter, plus 50g for the bean ragoût

1 garlic bulb, cloves peeled and crushed

4 tbsp chopped flat-leaf parsley leaves

sea salt and freshly ground black pepper

flavourless vegetable oil, to deep-fry

4 French-trimmed skinless chicken breasts (wing bones attached)

75g plain flour

3 eggs, lightly beaten

90g panko crumbs

125g runner beans, trimmed and cut into 4cm pieces

125g garden peas

4 spring onions, roughly chopped

125g broad beans, skins removed

6 garlic scapes, blanched, cut into 4cm pieces (optional)

Put the 175g of butter, all but one clove of the garlic and half the parsley into a bowl and beat together, then season with salt and black pepper. Spoon in a line on to a sheet of cling film and roll up into a log, then twist the end to secure and place in the fridge for one hour to set.

Heat a deep-fat fryer to 160°C/320°F or heat the oil for deep-frying in a deep heavy-based saucepan until a breadcrumb sizzles and turns brown when dropped into it. (CAUTION: hot oil can be dangerous. Do not leave unattended.)

Insert a knife horizontally into the bone end of the chicken breast, just next to the bone, and carefully move the knife from side to side, creating a pocket in the centre of the breast.

Slice the garlic butter into 1cm-thick fingers and place a few in each pocket, pressing in as far as possible.

Put the flour, eggs and panko crumbs into three separate shallow dishes. Season the flour. Pass the chicken through the flour, turning to coat all sides, then through the egg. Repeat, so each chicken breast has two coats of flour and egg. Finally roll each through the breadcrumbs to coat totally.

Carefully lower two at a time into the hot fat and fry for eight to 10 minutes until golden and the chicken has cooked through. Drain on kitchen paper and set aside to keep warm while you cook the rest.

Meanwhile, heat a sauté pan until medium hot, add the runner beans, 275ml of water and 25g of the remaining butter and bring to the boil. Add the peas, spring onions, garlic and broad beans and simmer for three or four minutes until all the vegetables are tender. Add the rest of the butter and parsley and the garlic scapes (if using) and heat through, then check the seasoning.

Spoon the vegetables into the centre of four plates, top with a chicken kiev and serve.

GRAN'S TOAD-IN-THE-HOLE WITH MY MUM'S ONION GRAVY

My gran's old recipe from her gran. Yes, it really does use eight eggs. This is the best Yorkshire pudding recipe there is. End of.

Serves 4–6

225g plain flour
8 eggs, lightly beaten
1 tbsp grainy mustard
570ml whole milk
sea salt
75g beef dripping or lard
6 good-quality sausages
2 onions, finely sliced
1–2 tbsp yeast extract
75ml red wine
1 tbsp gravy granules
200ml beef stock
knob of unsalted butter

Place the plain flour into a bowl and make a well in the centre.

Whisk in the eggs and mustard until just smooth, then gradually add the milk and a pinch of salt, whisking to a smooth batter.

Place in the fridge for at least four hours, preferably overnight.

Preheat the oven to 220°C/425°F/gas mark 7. Place three-quarters of the beef dripping into a roasting tin and place in the oven.

Heat a frying pan until hot, then add the remaining dripping and, when it's melted, add the sausages and cook, turning, until brown on each side.

Remove the batter from the fridge and whisk once more to combine.

Place the sausages in the roasting tin and pour over the batter.

Place in the oven for 30 minutes, then open the door and allow the steam to escape, then shut the door once more and cook for a final 10 minutes.

Meanwhile, make the gravy using the same pan that the sausages were cooked in. Place the pan back on the heat, add the onions and cook over a high heat for 10 minutes until just softened and browned.

Add the yeast extract and cook for one minute, then add the wine and cook until reduced by half. Whisk the gravy granules with a little water until smooth, then add 250ml of water and whisk once more.

Pour into the pan and cook for a few minutes, then add the stock and simmer for five minutes. Season to taste and keep warm until the toad is cooked, then whisk in the knob of butter to make it glossy.

Remove the toad from the oven and let it stand for a few minutes. Serve a large spoonful with a ladleful of gravy and some buttered peas.

CHICKEN WITH CHORIZO AND BEAN STEW

This is what I cook for myself: it is packed full of flavour and colour and – using chicken thighs – relatively cheap to make, too. Chorizo comes in many guises but look for the word 'picante' which means spicy. It will be full of paprika and perfect for this dish.

Serves 2

3 tbsp olive oil

40g unsalted butter

2 whole skin-on chicken legs, divided into drumsticks and thighs

2 shallots

1 lemon, halved

1 garlic bulb, halved horizontally

2 sprigs of rosemary

4 sprigs of thyme

200g chorizo, cut into small chunks

2 tomatoes, peeled, deseeded and finely chopped (see page 18)

1 x 660g jar of white haricot beans, drained and rinsed

250ml chicken stock

2 tbsp roughly chopped flat-leaf parsley leaves

sea salt and freshly ground black pepper

Preheat the oven to 220°C/425°F/gas mark 7.

Heat an ovenproof frying pan until hot, add half of both the olive oil and butter and, when it's foaming, add the chicken and fry until just golden on both sides.

Cut one shallot in half lengthways and add to the pan with the lemon and garlic, reserving 2 garlic cloves. Add half the sprigs of herbs. Place in the oven and roast for 15 minutes until golden and the chicken is cooked through. (Cut through the thickest piece to check: the juices should run clear with no trace of pink. If there is, cook for a few minutes longer, then check again.)

Meanwhile, finely chop the remaining shallot, reserved garlic cloves and the leaves from the remaining sprigs of herbs. Heat a sauté pan until medium hot, add the remaining olive oil and the chorizo and cook for five minutes, until the oil has changed colour and the chorizo is crispy around the edges. Add the tomatoes, chopped garlic and shallot and cook without colour for one minute. Add the beans, rosemary and thyme and sauté for two minutes.

Pour in the stock and bring to a simmer, then cook for four or five minutes until softened and the stock has slightly reduced.

Stir in the remaining butter and the parsley, seasoning to taste, especially with plenty of pepper.

Ladle the beans into the middle of soup plates, top with some chicken, then place a sautéed lemon half, shallot half and garlic bulb half alongside.

MACKEREL EN CROÛTE WITH GOOSEBERRY CHUTNEY

This was an idea we had in my restaurant in Malton. These are simple flavours and it is simple to make, too. Even better, these can be assembled in advance for the perfect dinner party dish, sort of a fishy sausage roll! Mackerel, even more than most fish, needs to be spanking fresh.

Get the fishmonger to remove the bones from the mackerel, but try to keep the fillets together or it may fall apart (that's why I leave the tail on).

Serves 4

For the chutney
125g caster sugar
50g sultanas
leaves from 2 sprigs of thyme
40g piece of root ginger, peeled and
    finely chopped
½ shallot, finely chopped
100ml cider vinegar
300g gooseberries, cleaned, topped and tailed
sea salt and freshly ground black pepper

For the mackerel
250g salmon fillet, skinned, pin-boned and
    roughly chopped
juice of 1 lemon
110ml double cream
4 mackerel, heads removed, gutted and deboned,
    tails left on (ask your fishmonger to do this)
leaves from 4 sprigs of tarragon
600g all-butter puff pastry, rolled to 5mm thick
2 eggs, lightly beaten
unsalted butter, for the foil

For the chutney, put the sugar into a heavy-based pan and heat, without stirring, until it has melted and turned to a golden-brown caramel, swirling the pan from time to time. Stir in the sultanas, thyme, ginger and shallot.

Add the cider vinegar and gooseberries, return to the heat and bring to the boil, then simmer gently for eight to 10 minutes until the gooseberries are soft, stirring occasionally. Season with salt and pepper and set aside to cool slightly.

To make the mackerel, preheat the oven to 220°C/425°F/gas mark 7.

Place the salmon fillet into a food processor with the lemon juice and blitz to a fine paste, then gradually add the cream with the processor still running until thickened. Season with salt and pepper.

Place the mackerel on their sides and open up the cavities, then stuff with the tarragon leaves and the salmon mousse, being careful, so that the fish doesn't tear.

Cut the pastry into 4 rectangles, each about 18cm x 15cm; the width should be about half the length of the fish, and the length long enough to wrap around the stuffed fish. Brush the pastry with egg, then wrap around the centre of the fish, overlapping the ends underneath.

Place on to a baking tray in a row, then mark the pastry with the end of an apple corer or similar to replicate fish scales and brush with egg. Wrap the tails in buttered foil to stop them from burning.

Sprinkle with some sea salt, then bake in the hot oven for 20 minutes until golden and cooked through. Remove from the oven and rest for five minutes.

Remove the foil from the tails, cut the fish in half and place the tail end upright on to serving plates, with the other half lying alongside. Finish with a dollop of gooseberry chutney.

BARBECUE BABY BACK RIBS
WITH CELERIAC SLAW

The crew couldn't wait to get stuck into these… but all good things come to those who wait and this recipe is the prime example, because the ribs are cooked for a long time. Some recipes tell you to cook ribs in sauce in the oven from raw. I find, cooked that way, they end up tough. The best way is to poach them first, so the meat just falls off the bones.

Serves 2–4

For the ribs

2kg racks of baby back pork ribs
2 celery sticks, halved
1 onion, thickly sliced
2 red chillies, split lengthways
1 garlic bulb, halved horizontally
250ml apple juice
125ml tomato ketchup
150g dark muscovado sugar
2 tbsp Worcestershire sauce
1 tsp smoked hot paprika
1 tsp smoked sweet paprika
75ml white wine vinegar
50ml bourbon whiskey

For the slaw

3 egg yolks
1 tbsp Dijon mustard
2 tbsp cider vinegar
300ml rapeseed oil
1 celeriac, peeled and julienned
2 tbsp roughly chopped flat-leaf parsley leaves
sea salt and freshly ground black pepper

Place the ribs into a large, wide saucepan, add the celery, onion, chillies, garlic and apple juice, then pour in enough water just to cover. Bring to the boil, then reduce the heat and simmer very gently for 1–1½ hours until tender, skimming off any scum from time to time.

Meanwhile, make the sauce. Heat a frying pan until hot, add the ketchup and muscovado sugar and cook for two or three minutes until it liquefies. Add the Worcestershire sauce, smoked paprikas and vinegar. Bring to the boil, then reduce the heat and simmer for five minutes until thickened. Add the bourbon, mix well, then set aside.

To make the slaw, whisk together the egg yolks, mustard and vinegar in a bowl or small processor. Still whisking, start adding the oil in a very thin trickle to make a mayonnaise; the mixture should be thick and light once the oils are incorporated.

Pour into a bowl, then stir in the celeriac and parsley and mix well. Season with salt and pepper.

When the ribs are done, preheat the oven to 240°C/475°F/gas mark 9, or as hot as it will go.

Lift the ribs out of the poaching liquor and place on a tray, then brush with the sauce on all sides. Roast the oven for 10–15 minutes, until charred around the edges and sticky, turning occasionally.

Pile on to a platter and serve the celeriac slaw and remaining sauce alongside.

SOUTHERN-FRIED BUTTERMILK CHICKEN WITH TOMATO AND SWEETCORN SALSA

Go on, you know you want to try it. Proper TV food: just pile it up in the centre of the table and watch everyone dive in. Once you have cooked it, you can change the spices to make it hotter if you want. Make sure the frying oil isn't too hot, or the coating will burn rather than turn deliciously brown.

Serves 3 – 4

For the chicken

400ml buttermilk

1 tsp sea salt

1 medium chicken, cut into 10 portions

125g plain flour

finely grated zest of 1 unwaxed lemon

1½ tsp smoked hot paprika

1½ tsp mustard powder

1½ tsp celery salt

1½ tsp dried thyme

1½ tsp dried oregano

2 tsp cracked black pepper

flavourless vegetable oil, to shallow-fry

For the salsa

90g caster sugar

300g tomatoes, finely chopped

2 red chillies, finely chopped

300g canned sweetcorn, drained and rinsed

2 tbsp red wine vinegar

juice of 1 lime

2 tbsp roughly chopped flat-leaf parsley leaves

Put the buttermilk and salt into a bowl and whisk to combine, then add the chicken and stir to coat. Cover and place in the fridge to marinate for at least four hours, preferably overnight.

Remove from the fridge and allow to come to room temperature. Preheat the oven to 200°C/400°F/gas mark 6.

Place the flour, lemon zest and all the spices into a bowl and toss together until well combined. Lift the chicken out of the buttermilk, scraping off as much of it as you can, then place into the spiced flour, tossing really well to coat all the pieces.

Heat a large ovenproof frying pan until hot, add enough oil to coat the bottom of the pan by 1cm, then add half the chicken, skin side down, and cook for two minutes on either side until golden. Place the whole pan in the oven for 15 minutes until the chicken is cooked through and the skin crispy. Cook the second batch, repeating the process. Take from the oven and place on kitchen paper to remove excess oil.

Meanwhile, for the salsa, heat a frying pan until hot, add the caster sugar and, without stirring, wait until it's a light golden caramel, swirling the pan occasionally. Add the chopped tomatoes and cook for one minute until just softened.

Add the chillies, sweetcorn, red wine vinegar, lime juice and parsley and cook for six to eight minutes until thickened and the tomato is all broken down. Season well with salt and pepper.

Pile the chicken on to a platter and serve the salsa alongside.

VENISON, CHICKEN LIVER AND ARMAGNAC TERRINE

A bit poncey calling this a terrine – that was the editor of the book as she lives in London – to you and me, it's a pâté, but a nice one at that. Once you've made it you will see how easy it is and, on the table for a party or lunch, it's a hit. I have it in the fridge and keep picking at it with bread and pickles (yeah, I know, kitchen pickers wear big knickers, but it's lovely).

Serves 6 – 8

350g venison fillet, cut into 2cm-wide strips
350g chicken livers
sea salt and freshly ground black pepper
2 tbsp rapeseed oil, plus more for the foil
2 tbsp armagnac
550g rashers of streaky bacon
300g skinless boneless chicken breasts, roughly chopped
200ml double cream
50g toasted chopped hazelnuts
50g dried cranberries
2 tbsp finely chopped tarragon leaves

Season the venison and chicken livers with salt and pepper, then heat a large frying pan and add the rapeseed oil. When the oil is hot, add the venison a few pieces at a time and seal on each side, then set aside. Repeat with the chicken livers, then – standing well back and protecting your forearms – pour in the armagnac and set it on fire with a match. When the flames die down, set aside.

While these cool, use the bacon to line a 1kg loaf tin, overlapping the rashers in the base a little and leaving about 5cm of their lengths falling over the edge of the tin on each side. Preheat the oven to 180°C/350°F/gas mark 4.

Place the chicken breast into a food processor and blitz to a fine purée, then add the double cream and blitz to combine. Season with plenty of salt and pepper, then tip into a bowl and fold in the hazelnuts and cranberries.

Scoop one-third of the chicken mixture into the prepared tin, then top with the venison. Layer on another one-third of the chicken mixture, then the tarragon, chicken livers and their juices. Finish with the remaining chicken mixture, then fold the bacon over the top to cover all the filling.

Oil a piece of foil and place over the top of the tin, then seal tightly around the edges and place into a deep tray. Half fill the tray with hot water then place into the oven for 1¼–1½ hours.

To check that the terrine is cooked, insert a skewer into the centre, then run it against the inside of your wrist: if it's piping hot, it's cooked through. If not, return it to the oven and cook for another 10 minutes, then check again.

Remove from the oven and allow to cool completely before placing in the fridge to chill.

To serve, turn out of the mould and cut into slices. Serve with gherkins and some charred bread.

THE ULTIMATE BURGER

Burgers are about great meat, seasoning and nothing else… well, that's what I learned while in America. I worked in one of the oldest diners in the US; the menu was the size of the Bible and it ended up being a bit of a joke trying to pick something to eat! But the burger was the reason the diner was still there after all that time. Served in a brioche bun with home-made mayo, this is the business. Proper home comfort food. And a quick note to the blokes: if you're considering this recipe, don't burn it on the bloody barbecue like you do everything else.

Serves 4

800g minced beef steak
sea salt and freshly ground black pepper
3 egg yolks
1 tbsp Dijon mustard
300ml rapeseed oil
25g beer or whole grain mustard
juice of ½ lemon
2 tbsp vegetable oil
4 brioche rolls, halved
4 tbsp mild chilli relish
½ round lettuce, leaves separated
2 tomatoes, sliced
200g cheese slices, preferably Monterey Jack
8 gherkins, sliced
1 red onion, sliced

Put the minced meat in a large bowl and season with salt and pepper, then divide into four and form into patties. Set on a plate, cover and place in the fridge for one hour to firm up.

Meanwhile, prepare your barbecue (if using) so the flames have died down and the coals are just glowing.

Whisk together the egg yolks and mustard then, still whisking, start adding the rapeseed oil in a very thin trickle to make a mayonnaise; the mixture should be thick yet light once all the oil is incorporated. Stir in the beer mustard and lemon juice and season to taste with salt and pepper.

Rub the patties with the vegetable oil, then place on the barbecue and chargrill on each side for three or four minutes. (Alternatively cook over a high heat on a griddle pan.) Place each brioche cut side down on to the barbecue and cook for one minute, then set aside.

To assemble the burger, place some relish on the base of each bun, top with lettuce, tomatoes, the burger, cheese, mustard mayo, gherkins and red onion, then top with the bun lids.

Place the burgers on serving plates and secure with wooden skewers to keep them together, if you like.

I was brought up on a farm and some of the recipes here are our old family favourites. But there are also new dishes from my restaurant, such as the beef dish that food critic Jay Rayner said was the best he had eaten in 2013. I've stripped it back to make it easier to make at home, but it will be a hit at any dinner party.

Slow comforts

BRAISED BEEF CHEEKS WITH BEER AND MASH

These require a long time to cook properly and they look a fair size when raw, but will shrink when cooked. I love them with a simple glazed carrot and mash at home, though we trick the dish up a bit in the restaurant and it's our biggest seller. I hope you like them, as beef cheeks are one of the best-tasting pieces of meat you can buy.

Serves 4 (Yorkshire portions)

For the beef

4 large beef cheeks
2 onions, roughly chopped
5 carrots, peeled, 4 left whole, 1 cut into chunks
1 garlic bulb, halved horizontally
3 sprigs of thyme
2 x 500ml bottles of porter ale
sea salt and freshly ground black pepper
2 tbsp olive oil
150g unsalted butter
750ml beef stock
5 star anise
50g caster sugar

For the mash

1kg floury potatoes, peeled and cut into chunks
150g unsalted butter
150ml double cream

Place the beef cheeks in a large bowl, add the onions, chopped carrot, garlic and thyme, pour over the beer and place in the fridge for at least 12 hours.

Preheat the oven to 150°C/300°F/gas mark 2. Lift the beef cheeks out from the vegetables, pat dry, then season with salt and pepper.

Heat a large casserole dish until hot, add the olive oil and a knob of the butter and, when foaming, add two of the beef cheeks and sear on each side until browned. Remove and set aside. Repeat to cook the other two.

Return all the beef to the pan, add the vegetables and beer from the marinade and pour in the stock.

Bring to a simmer then part-cover with the casserole lid, leaving a 1cm gap at the side. Place into the oven for four or five hours.

Half an hour before the beef is ready, place the potatoes into a pan of cold, salted water and bring to the boil. Reduce the heat and simmer for 12–15 minutes, or until tender. Make the mash as on page 59.

Meanwhile, put the whole carrots, star anise, 100g of the butter and the sugar into a pan and add enough water to just cover, with some salt. Set over a low heat and cook for 20–30 minutes, until tender and glazed.

Remove the casserole from the oven and strain the sauce into a saucepan. Place over a medium heat and cook until reduced and thick enough to just coat the back of a spoon.

Whisk in the remaining butter until the sauce is shiny, then season with salt and pepper.

Lift out a beef cheek and place on a soup plate. Spoon the mash alongside, add a glazed carrot, then generously ladle on the sauce.

SALT CRUST DOUGH-BAKED CELERIAC WITH CRÈME FRAÎCHE AND CHIVE DRESSING

Looks weird, I know, and while you're making it you might feel the same… but good things will come of it in the end. Salt crust cooking is nothing new; from fish to veg, most things can be cooked this way and you will be amazed at the flavour it creates, seasoning as it cooks. Vegetarians will love the simple flavours and it's good hot or cold. You have to serve it simply as you want the flavour to come through. I use it for dinner parties at mine; it's a good talking point.

Serves 4

500g strong white bread flour
200g fine sea salt
4 egg whites
2 medium or 1 large celeriac, washed thoroughly
100g crème fraîche
2 tbsp extra virgin olive oil
freshly ground black pepper
3 tbsp finely chopped chives
50g watercress, coarse stalks removed
handful of chive flowers (optional)

Place the flour and salt into a large bowl or food mixer and mix until combined, then add the egg whites and 100–125ml of water and mix for about five minutes, until it forms a soft, smooth dough.

Remove and flatten into a 2cm-thick disc, wrap in cling film and chill in the fridge for 30 minutes.

Preheat the oven to 180°C/350°F/gas mark 4. Roll out the dough to about 1cm thick. Set aside a small piece. Place a celeriac in the centre of each half of dough, or just use the whole piece for a big one, and wrap to cover totally. Use the trimmings to make a 'string' (see right).

Place on a baking tray and roast in the oven for 1–1½ hours or until the pastry is hard and the celeriac tender; to check if it's tender, insert a skewer into the centre, there should be very little resistance.

Meanwhile, make the dressing: whisk the crème fraîche and olive oil together in a bowl then season well with pepper and stir in the chives (or scatter the chives separately). Set aside in the fridge until ready to use.

When the celeriac is tender, remove and cool slightly before cracking the pastry off.

Finely slice the celeriac and lay across a serving plate, then drizzle the dressing over the top, add the chives if you didn't stir them into the crème fraîche and arrange the watercress and chive flowers (if using) on top.

You can cook most vegetables this way, carrots or small potatoes from my garden are great baked under a salt crust.

TARTIFLETTE AND
BACON FAT SALAD

*I'm not into skiing, although I did try it once and – apart from nearly
breaking my leg – I also took out seven school kids and a fence.
I haven't and wouldn't do it again. You should stop wearing things
on your feet other than shoes and slippers after the age of five. The
French Alps are good for some things though, including tartiflette.*

Serves 6–8

*1.5kg red-skinned potatoes, such as Desiree,
   well scrubbed*

75g unsalted butter, plus more to brush

1 large onion, finely sliced

2 sprigs of thyme

1 garlic clove

*10 thick rashers of smoked dry-cured
   streaky bacon*

*250g whole petit Reblochon cheese,
   rind removed*

sea salt and freshly ground black pepper

1 tsp Dijon mustard

1½ tbsp white wine vinegar

1 egg yolk

2 tbsp vegetable oil

100g mixed salad leaves

Preheat the oven to 200°C/400°F/gas mark 6.

Place the potatoes into a large pan and bring to the boil in their skins. Cook for 10 minutes.

Meanwhile, heat a frying pan until medium hot, add a knob of the butter, the onion and thyme and cook for five to eight minutes until softened, but not coloured at all.

Drain the potatoes and, when they are cool enough, scrape off the skins with a table knife. Cut into slices around 5mm thick.

Take an ovenproof dish, cut the garlic in half and rub the cut side all over the dish, then smear on some butter.

Lay the onion into the dish and spread out over the base, then lay six rashers of bacon across that. Lay the potatoes in concentric circles over the top, then place the cheese in the centre.

Dot with half the remaining butter, pepper and a touch of salt and place in the oven for 45 minutes, until the potatoes are lovely and crisp at the edges and the cheese is totally melted.

Meanwhile, melt most of the remaining butter in a frying pan and chop the remaining four rashers of bacon into lardons. Add to the pan and cook over a medium heat until the fat starts to render, then increase the heat and cook until crisp and browned. Remove with a slotted spoon and place on kitchen paper.

Whisk the Dijon mustard, vinegar and egg yolk together until paler, then whisk in the vegetable oil to emulsify. Pour into the hot fat in the bacon pan and whisk until thickened and cooled slightly. Check the seasoning. Toss the crispy bacon with the salad leaves, then dress with a little dressing.

Remove the tartiflette from the oven, melt the remaining butter in a small saucepan and brush the tartiflette with the melted butter. Serve with the salad.

ROAST PEPPERED BEEF WITH BOURBON MUSTARD AND ALL THE TRIMMINGS

Making your own mustard is so easy to do and mixing in other flavours such as beer gives it a different appeal. If you blend it for longer, the mixture will turn as smooth as French mustard. You do have to start it the day before, ideally, and the Yorkshire batter will benefit from being rested overnight, too.

Serves 6 – 8

For the Yorkshire puddings
225g plain flour
sea salt and freshly ground black pepper
8 eggs
600ml whole milk
50g beef dripping or lard

For the beef
50g yellow mustard seeds
50g brown mustard seeds
75g light soft brown sugar
2 tbsp runny honey
100ml cider vinegar
75ml bourbon whiskey
4kg 3-bone forerib of 28-day-aged beef,
    at room temperature
a little flavourless vegetable oil
300ml beef stock

For the roast potatoes
10 King Edward potatoes, peeled and cut
    into 2 or 3
50g lard, beef dripping or vegetable oil

For the Yorkshire puddings, place the flour into a bowl and season. Add the eggs and whisk to a batter. Pour in the milk and whisk until smooth, then place in the fridge for at least one hour, but preferably overnight.

Place the mustard seeds, sugar, honey and 3 tbsp of water into a saucepan and bring to a simmer. Turn the heat off and add the vinegar. Put the mixture into a large bowl, cover and set aside for at least four hours, or overnight. The seeds will absorb all the liquid.

Pour everything into a blender with the bourbon and blitz until the mustard becomes creamy, but leave it slightly grainy. Season.

For the beef, preheat the oven to 200°C/400°F/gas mark 6. Season the beef with plenty of pepper. Heat a large frying pan until very hot, then add a little oil and fry the beef on all sides until browned. Put it in a roasting dish, then spread some of the mustard all over the beef and season with salt. Roast for 1½ hours.

Place the potatoes into a large saucepan, cover with water, add a pinch of salt and bring to the boil. Simmer for one minute. Drain into a colander and shake around a little to rough up the edges. Set a deep

roasting tray on a medium heat and add the fat. Add the potatoes and fry on each side until they start to brown. Sprinkle with salt and place in the oven with the beef for the last 30 minutes of cooking time, until starting to turn golden and crispy.

Remove the beef from the oven, cover with foil and rest for 30 minutes. Turn the potatoes, increase the oven temperature to 220°C/425°F/gas mark 7 and cook for a further 20–30 minutes, while the beef rests. Set the roasting pan over a medium heat until bubbling, then add the stock and cook until reduced by half, then season.

At the same time, divide the dripping or lard between 2 x 12 hole muffin tins or Yorkshire tins. Place in the oven for 10 minutes until smoking hot. Whisk the batter, then carefully pour it into the tins, filling each hole two-thirds full. Place into the oven for 20 minutes (do not open the door during this time). If the roast potatoes are done, take them out and keep them warm.

After 20 minutes, open the oven door to allow any steam to escape, then reduce the temperature to 190°C/375°F/gas mark 5. Cook for 15 minutes until golden and crispy.

Carve the beef. Pile everything on to platters so everyone helps themselves.

TARRAGON-STUFFED CROWN OF LAMB WITH DUCHESS POTATOES

This stuffing comes from my time with the Roux Brothers. It's a great recipe and, with the lamb, makes a wonderful combination. I cook it on the barbecue at home, but 30–40 minutes in a hot oven will do the trick. It makes it into this 'slow' chapter, though, because there's a bit of work and faffing about to do before you get to the cooking stage.

Serves 4 – 6

For the lamb

1 small onion
25g unsalted butter, plus more for the foil
300g button mushrooms
leaves from 1 small bunch of tarragon, finely chopped
50g fresh white breadcrumbs
75g minced lamb
sea salt and freshly ground black pepper
2 x 7-bone French-trimmed racks of lamb

For the potatoes

4 large baking potatoes
25g unsalted butter
3 egg yolks

Preheat the oven to 200°C/400°F/gas mark 6. Bake the potatoes for 1–1¼ hours, until tender when pierced with a knife. When they're ready, blitz the onion in a food processor until very finely chopped. Heat a frying pan until warm, add the butter and onion and sweat for a couple of minutes.

Add the mushrooms to the processor and blitz to a really fine purée, then add them to the frying pan and increase the heat to high. Fry for two or three minutes until all the moisture has been driven off.

Tip into a bowl and add the tarragon, breadcrumbs and minced lamb. Season with salt and plenty of pepper.

Rub some butter over a sheet of foil and place it on a baking sheet. Make nicks in each rack of lamb, between each chop, on the opposite side to the fat of the chops. The cuts should be only 1–2cm deep. Stand both racks of lamb upright, bones in the air, fat sides together. Curve them around; the nicks you made should open slightly to allow you to form a circle with the two racks, fat-side inwards. Tie with kitchen string, fairly firmly. Pile the stuffing in the centre, packing it well.

Cook in the oven for 30–40 minutes, then remove and rest for 10 minutes before carving.

Meanwhile, when the potatoes are cool enough to handle, scoop out the flesh and pass it through a fine sieve into a bowl. Beat to a smooth and fluffy purée, then add the butter and egg yolks and check the seasoning.

Spoon into a piping bag, then pipe little pyramids on to a baking tray. When the lamb comes out of the oven to rest, place the duchess potatoes in the oven and bake for five to 10 minutes until golden brown,

Carve the lamb and serve with the stuffing and duchess potatoes.

CHICKEN CHASSEUR WITH CREAMY MASH

This is an old school dish that has fallen out of fashion, but who cares about that? It should be on every restaurant menu as it tastes so good. And it can easily be made at home. The vital thing is to use fresh tarragon, it tastes miles better than dried.

Serves 4

For the chicken

1.5kg whole chicken, jointed into 8
sea salt and freshly ground black and
  white pepper
1 tbsp plain flour
2 tbsp olive oil
110g unsalted butter
110g smoked streaky bacon, sliced into lardons
125g shallots, thickly sliced
150g chestnut mushrooms, halved if large
2 tbsp tomato purée
175ml white wine
400ml chicken stock
leaves from a small bunch of tarragon
3 tomatoes, skinned, deseeded and finely
  chopped (see page 18)
2 tbsp finely chopped flat-leaf parsley leaves

For the mash

1kg floury potatoes, peeled and cut into chunks
150g unsalted butter
150ml double cream

Season the chicken with salt and pepper then toss in the flour to coat.

Heat a large sauté pan until hot, add the oil, a knob of the butter and half the chicken pieces and fry skin side down for three or four minutes until golden. Turn and fry on the other side for another one or two minutes, then remove from the pan. Repeat with another knob of butter and the remaining chicken.

Add another knob of butter and the bacon and fry until golden brown, then add the shallots, mushrooms and tomato purée and fry for another couple of minutes.

Pour in the wine and bring to a simmer, stirring to deglaze the pan. Add the stock, then return the chicken to the pan with half the tarragon and bring to the boil.

Reduce the heat to a simmer, cover and cook for 30–40 minutes until the chicken is tender and the liquid slightly reduced.

Roughly chop the remaining tarragon. Add the tomatoes, parsley and tarragon to the pan, then check the seasoning and adjust it if needed.

Meanwhile, place the potatoes into a pan of salted water and bring to the boil. Reduce the heat and simmer for 12–15 minutes until tender. Make the mash as on page 59.

Serve each person with two pieces of chicken, with the sauce spooned over and a dollop of mash.

WEEPING LAMB WITH BOULANGÈRE POTATOES AND HOME-MADE MINT SAUCE

If there is one dish that got eaten up more qiuckly than any on the shoot, it was this one. The idea is that the lamb fat and juices drip on to the dish of potatoes cooking below it at the same time. The name of these potatoes comes from the baker's oven in which they were once cooked in villages all over France. The locals would use the oven heat leftover from bread baking to cook the spuds.

Serves 8

2.7kg leg of lamb
3–4 garlic cloves, cut into slivers
3 big sprigs of rosemary
1 tbsp olive oil
sea salt and freshly ground black pepper
6 large potatoes, peeled and thinly sliced
4 onions, thinly sliced
75g unsalted butter
500ml chicken stock
750ml good red wine
1 litre beef stock
75ml malt vinegar
pinch of caster sugar
leaves from a large bunch of mint, finely chopped

Preheat the oven to 200°C/400°F/gas mark 6. Using a small sharp knife, make a series of small deep slits about 4cm apart all over the leg of lamb and insert a sliver of garlic and a spriglet of rosemary, pressing right down.

Drizzle with the olive oil, add a good sprinkling of salt, then set aside while you build the potato dish.

Layer the potatoes and onions into a large ovenproof tray, seasoning each layer with salt and black pepper and finishing with potatoes. Dot with 50g of the butter, then pour over the chicken stock and press down lightly.

Put the roasting dish into the bottom of the oven and place the lamb on a small trivet on the oven rack directly above the potatoes.

Leave to roast for 1½ hours until the potatoes are cooked through, pressing the potatoes down into the cooking liquid every 30 minutes as it cooks.

Meanwhile, make the gravy: pour the red wine and beef stock into a sauté pan and set over a medium heat, bring to a simmer and cook for 30–45 minutes until reduced by three-quarters, thickened and glossy. Whisk in the last 25g of butter, check the seasoning and adjust it if needed.

Heat the malt vinegar and sugar in a pan until just simmering, then add the mint and stir until wilted. Taste and add salt, if you want.

Remove the meat from the oven and rest for 15 minutes before carving.

Carve the lamb and serve with the potatoes, gravy and mint sauce.

MUTTON HOTPOT WITH HERITAGE CARROTS

HRH the Prince of Wales is one of the biggest supporters of mutton in the UK. I've even done a dinner at his place using it. Mutton is one of those meats that people need to try and, when you do, you will realise how good it tastes. Like most things in this chapter it needs long cooking and is even better reheated on the second day.

Serves 4

2 mutton kidneys, fat on

1kg boneless leg of mutton, cut into 2.5cm pieces

2 tbsp plain flour

2 large onions, thickly sliced

2 bay leaves

2 tsp Worcestershire sauce

600ml beef stock

900g potatoes, peeled and cut into 5mm-thick slices

sea salt and freshly ground black pepper

100g unsalted butter, plus more to glaze (optional)

300g carrots, ideally heritage carrots, cleaned and trimmed

Preheat the oven to 180°C/350°F/gas mark 4.

Trim the kidneys of fat, then chop them into largish pieces. Place the kidney fat into a large ovenproof casserole pan and heat over a medium heat until it has rendered down. Meanwhile, toss the kidneys and mutton in the flour and shake off any excess. Add half the mutton leg and kidneys to the casserole and cook until browned on each side, then remove and set aside.

Add the remaining meat and cook again until browned on each side, then set aside. Now layer in half the onions and a bay leaf. Make another layer with all the mutton, then the last of the onions and the remaining bay leaf. Add the Worcestershire sauce and stock and bring to a simmer.

Arrange the potato slices on top in an overlapping pattern. Season the potatoes and add a few dots of butter over the surface. Cover with a tight-fitting lid and cook for two hours.

At the end of cooking, you can remove the lid, brush the potatoes with a little more butter, then place under the grill to glaze up if you like. Otherwise, just remove the lid and increase the oven temperature during the last 30 minutes of cooking time.

When it is cooked, bring a pan of salted water to the boil, add the carrots and simmer until just tender, three to five minutes. Drain and toss with the remaining butter, salt and pepper.

Serve a helping of hotpot with some carrots alongside.

LAMB SHANKS PIE

When I was younger and worked in London, we used to buy lamb shanks for 15p each. But, thanks to us chefs using them more, the price has gone up. They are still cheap given the amount of meat on them, but they need to be well cooked so it falls off the bone. They can also be bought in most supermarkets nowadays, which is an added bonus.

The key is make sure the shanks are cooked well and cooled before making the pie, that way the meat will just fall apart.

Serves 4

4 lamb shanks
sea salt and freshly ground black pepper
1 tbsp rapeseed oil
2 onions, roughly chopped
4 garlic cloves, crushed
2 tbsp plain flour, plus more to dust
250ml white wine
750ml chicken stock
600g potatoes, peeled and cut into
  2.5cm chunks
3 large carrots, peeled and cut into
  2.5cm chunks
4 celery sticks, cut into 2.5cm chunks
2 bay leaves
2 sprigs of rosemary
4 sprigs of thyme
400g can of haricot beans, drained
1 egg and 1 egg yolk, lightly beaten
400g rough puff pastry (for home-made,
  see page 74)
300g peas

Preheat the oven to 170°C/340°F/gas mark 3½.

Season the lamb shanks with salt and pepper. Heat a large casserole dish until hot, add the rapeseed oil and the lamb shanks and seal, turning, until golden brown on all sides. Remove and set aside, then add the onions. Cook for two or three minutes until softened, then add the garlic and cook for another minute. Add the flour, stir well and cook out for another minute before adding the white wine, stock, potatoes, carrots, celery, bay leaves, rosemary and thyme to the casserole. Bring to a simmer.

Stir in the beans, then return the lamb shanks to the pan and return to a gentle simmer. Cover and place in the oven for two hours, or simmer over a low heat on the hob if you prefer, until the lamb shanks are tender.

Remove from the oven. The lamb should be totally tender, but not quite falling off the bone. Place them upright in a baking dish with the vegetables around them, then set aside to cool completely. The lamb must be cold before you put the pastry on.

Preheat the oven to 180°C/350°F/gas mark 4.

Brush the sides of a pie dish with egg wash, inside and out. Roll the pastry out on a floured surface to 5cm bigger than the pie dish and 5mm thick.

Lay the sheet of pastry over the lamb shanks. Make four small slits with a sharp knife where the bones are and press gently down so that the bones stick out through the pastry. Crimp the pastry around the rim of the dish; this will help it stay attached and not slide off the dish. Brush with the egg and season with a little salt, then place in the oven and bake for 45–60 minutes until the pastry is golden brown and cooked through and the filling hot.

Bring a pan of salted water to the boil, add the peas and cook for three or four minutes until tender. Drain and serve with the pie.

BEEF RIBS WITH BARBECUE SAUCE, JACKET POTATOES AND CHIVE CREAM

Most of the time, 'ribs' means pork ribs but, every once in a while, you can find beef ribs at a butcher. Buy them. They are off the scale in terms of flavour and appearance. We use them in the restaurant, but they are simple to prepare and eat, with one big bone and tons of meat. I make these when my mates are over watching the Grand Prix.

Serves 4–6

For the beef ribs and jacket potatoes

4 'Jacob's ladder' beef ribs, sometimes known
   as short ribs
1 onion, chopped
1 garlic bulb, halved horizontally
1 tsp fennel seeds
2 star anise
4 baking potatoes
a little olive oil
sea salt and freshly ground black pepper
200ml double cream
juice of 1 lemon
2 tbsp finely chopped chives

For the barbecue sauce

25g unsalted butter, plus more for the potatoes
1 onion, roughly chopped
2 red chillies, finely sliced, deseeded or not, to
   taste (leaving the seeds in makes it hotter)
1 tsp fennel seeds, crushed
2 star anise
150g light muscovado sugar
300g tomato ketchup
150g chipotle chilli ketchup
150ml dark soy sauce

Place the ribs into a large, wide saucepan. Just-cover with water and add the onion, garlic, fennel seeds and star anise. Bring to the boil, then reduce the heat and simmer very gently for three hours until tender, skimming off any scum occasionally. Remove with a slotted spoon and pat dry with kitchen paper.

When the meat has been simmered for two hours, preheat the oven to 200°C/400°F/gas mark 6. Rub the baking potatoes with a little oil then place on a small pile of sea salt on a baking tray. Bake in the oven for 1½ hours, or until tender.

Meanwhile, make the sauce. Heat a sauté pan until hot, add the butter and onion and fry for four or five minutes until softened.

Add the chillies, fennel seeds, star anise and sugar and cook for a further three or four minutes, until the sugar has dissolved. Add both ketchups and the soy sauce and bring to the boil, then reduce the heat and simmer for five minutes until thickened.

Remove from the heat and cool slightly, then place in a blender and purée until smooth.

Dip the ribs into the sauce, then place into a baking tray and spoon some more sauce over the top.

Bake in the oven alongside the potatoes for their last 15–20 minutes of cooking time, until sticky.

While the ribs cook, put the double cream, lemon juice, chives and a pinch of salt into a large bowl and whisk until thickened.

Serve the ribs with the jacket potatoes topped with a dollop of butter and the chive cream.

HOME-MADE PUFF PASTRY WILD BOAR SAUSAGE ROLLS

Wild boar are amazing creatures and, with my background on a pig farm, they are very interesting to me. Jody Scheckter at Laverstoke Park introduced me to the joys of eating wild boar, as he produces them. He barbecues all year round, even in the depths of winter – you have to forgive him as he's South African and that's what they do – and serves these sausage rolls. They are delicious with a cold beer. Double the recipe if you're having a big party.

Serves 4 – 6

For the puff pastry

250g plain flour, plus more to dust
pinch of fine salt
300g unsalted butter, 50g cut into cubes, the
   rest left in a block

For the filling

25g unsalted butter
1 onion, chopped
3 garlic cloves, chopped
50ml brandy
500g minced wild boar
leaves from 6 sprigs of tarragon,
   roughly chopped
sea salt and freshly ground black pepper
2 egg yolks, lightly beaten

Start with the puff pastry. Put the flour and salt into a bowl with the cubes of butter and rub together with your fingertips to form crumbs, then stir in 150ml of cold water and mix to form a soft dough. Pat out to form a 2cm-thick rectangle.

Put the block of butter between two pieces of greaseproof paper and bash out with a rolling pin to a rectangle measuring about 15 x 10cm.

Lightly flour a work surface, roll the dough out to form another rectangle, this time 30 x 20cm, then remove the butter from the papers and place in the centre of the dough. Fold one side of the dough over the butter, then fold the other side over to meet it, covering the butter. Pinch together the dough at the top and bottom to seal the butter inside, then fold it in half lengthways.

Turn 90°, then roll out again to a 30 x 20cm rectangle. Fold one-quarter of the dough across to the centre, then fold the other side over to meet it. Fold in half lengthways, then repeat the process one more time. Cover and place in the fridge to chill for one hour.

Meanwhile, make the filling. Heat a frying pan until medium hot, add the butter, onions and garlic and sweat for five minutes, until softened. Add the

brandy, then stand back while you set light to the pan. When the flames die down, tip into a large bowl to cool.

When the onions are cold, add the minced wild boar and tarragon and mix, then season generously.

Preheat the oven to 230°C/450°F/ gas mark 8. Line a baking tray with baking parchment.

Lightly flour a work surface, then roll out the pastry into a 40 x 30cm rectangle about 5mm thick. Cut the rectangle in half so you have two 40 x 15cm rectangles of pastry.

Divide the sausage mixture into two and place in a line lengthways down each sheet of pastry towards one side. Brush the long edges of the pastry with the beaten egg. Fold the pastry over to cover the filling, crimp the edge, then trim to straighten. Place on the prepared baking tray, seam sides down, then brush once more with egg.

Place in the oven and cook for 20–30 minutes until golden brown and cooked through.

Cut each sausage roll into pieces, pile on to a plate and serve hot or cold.

CHESTNUT, SAGE AND ONION-STUFFED PORK WITH DAUPHINOISE POTATOES

You really have to buy this piece of meat from a butcher as the belly needs to be attached to the loin. Rolling it up with the stuffing will make for one massive joint for a feast but, when cooked – trust me – there will be very little left. Cooking it for a long time will make the crackling nice and crisp.

Serves 12–16

For the pork

2 onions, roughly chopped
75g unsalted butter
400g cooked chestnuts, roughly chopped
leaves from 1 large bunch of sage, finely sliced
300g fresh white breadcrumbs
sea salt and freshly ground black pepper
5.5kg boneless loin of pork, with the
    belly attached

For the dauphinoise potatoes

2 garlic cloves, halved
75g unsalted butter
2kg King Edward potatoes, peeled and
    thinly sliced
pinch of freshly grated nutmeg
600ml double cream
600ml whole milk

Preheat the oven to 150°C/300°F/gas mark 2.

Put the onions into a food processor and blitz until they are finely chopped. Heat a frying pan until medium hot, add 25g of the butter and, when it's foaming, add the onions and cook for five minutes until just softened.

Put the chestnuts, sage and breadcrumbs into a bowl with the onions, season with plenty of salt and pepper, then mix well.

Lay the pork, flesh side up, on a chopping board, with the belly flap facing away from you.

With a sharp knife, make an incision in the eye of the loin halfway down, running parallel to the board and cutting almost all the way through. Open the loin up and repeat a few times, cutting so the loin opens up and lies as flat as the belly part of the pork.

Season with salt and pepper, spread the stuffing out along the loin, then roll up into a large sausage.

Secure with string at five or six points along the loin, then transfer to a roasting tin. Rub the rest of the butter (50g) over the top of the pork and season with plenty of salt.

Put into the oven and roast for five hours. After the pork has cooked for 4¼ hours, increase the oven temperature to 200°C/400°F/gas mark 6. Assemble the potatoes. Rub an ovenproof dish with the cut sides of the garlic, then rub about 1 tsp of the butter around the inside and place the potatoes in the dish in layers, overlapping a little, until the dish is just full, seasoning with salt, pepper and nutmeg as you layer.

Pour the cream and milk over the potatoes to cover, then season, dot with the remaining butter, cover tightly with foil and place in the oven for 30 minutes.

Remove the meat. By now the crackling should be crisp and the pork very tender. Rest for 30 minutes (it should have cooked for five hours in total). Remove the foil from the potatoes and cook for another 30 minutes until tender.

Carve the pork into slices and serve with its pan juices and the potatoes.

BEEF AND MUSTARD PIE

Everyone loves a pie and this is one dish that epitomises home comfort food for me. And if you want to know what to cook a chef when they come round for dinner, then cook them a pie.

Serves 4–6

1kg beef skirt, cut into large chunks
2 tbsp plain flour
sea salt and freshly ground black pepper
2 tbsp rapeseed oil
2 tbsp whole grain mustard
200ml red wine
400ml beef stock
1 onion, finely sliced
2 large carrots, cut into 2.5cm pieces
3 sprigs of thyme
2 egg yolks, lightly beaten
400g all-butter puff pastry, rolled 5mm thick
  (for home-made, see page 111)
300g fine green beans
25g unsalted butter

Preheat the oven to 150°C/300°F/gas mark 2.

Toss the beef and flour together in a bowl with salt and pepper.

Heat a large casserole dish until hot, add half the rapeseed oil and enough of the beef to just cover the bottom of the casserole.

Fry until browned on each side, then remove and set aside. Repeat with the remaining oil and beef in batches.

Return all the beef to the pan, add the mustard, pour in the wine and cook until reduced by half. Now pour in the stock and add the onion, carrots and thyme and season well. Cover and place in the oven for two hours. Check the seasoning and set aside to cool.

When the beef is cold, place it in a 30cm pie dish. Preheat the oven to 200°C/400°F/gas mark 6. Brush the edge of the dish with the egg. Trim a 2.5cm-wide strip from the pastry and stick this on to the dish all the way around, to create something for the pastry top to stick to. Lay the pastry on top.

Cut around the edge, leaving just enough pastry to crimp at the edges, and brush with the egg. Bake in the oven for 30 minutes until the pastry is golden brown and cooked through.

When ready to eat, bring a saucepan of salted water to the boil, add the beans and cook for four or five minutes, until just tender. Drain and toss with the butter and some pepper.

Place a large spoonful of pie on to each plate with some green beans alongside.

SPELT BREAD-CRUSTED HAM

I had this idea while in the States. They served something similar in a smaller portion – which is unlike them – but I've made it with a large piece. The idea is, when its cooked with the bread topping, you just dive in and then the bread is used to mop up the ham juices.

Serves 8 –10

For the ham and vegetables

1 raw ham, about 4–6kg, bone in, soaked overnight if necessary (check with your butcher)

2 onions, cut into thick slices

1 carrot, cut into big chunks

2 bay leaves

10 black peppercorns

600g potatoes, peeled and cut into large chunks

8 spring onions, trimmed

350g runner beans, trimmed and cut in half

300g fresh peas

small handful of sprigs of mint, torn in half

small handful of sprigs of flat-leaf parsley,
 torn in half

1 egg, lightly beaten

For the spelt bread

1kg spelt flour, plus more to dust

2 tsp caster sugar

2 tsp salt

2 x 7g sachets of fast-action yeast

700ml water

Place the ham into a large saucepan, add the onions, carrot, bay leaves and peppercorns then cover with cold water. Bring to the boil rapidly, skim off any scum that rises to the top, reduce the heat, cover and simmer for about 20 minutes per 500g; it will take 3–4 hours, depending on size.

To check the ham is cooked, insert a skewer into its centre, then run it against the inside of your wrist: if it's piping hot, it's cooked. Remove from the heat and cool totally in the liquid.

Meanwhile, put the flour, sugar and salt into a large bowl or a food mixer fitted with a dough hook. Put the yeast into a jug with 200ml of the water and mix to combine, then turn on the mixer and slowly add the yeast water, then measure in the rest of the water to the jug and add gradually to the dough, making sure you've pulled all the flour into the dough.

Tip out on to a very lightly floured work surface then knead well for five to 10 minutes until elastic. Place into a large bowl, cover and set aside to double in size, about two hours.

Preheat the oven to 180°C/350°F/ gas mark 4. Remove the ham from the stock and discard the vegetables, reserving the stock. Carefully peel off the ham skin and discard.

Place the potatoes, spring onions, beans, peas and mint and parsley sprigs into a large ovenproof casserole big enough to fit the ham in. Pour over 1.25 litres of the reserved ham stock (use the rest for a soup), then place the ham on top. Brush the outside edge of the casserole with the beaten egg.

Lift the dough out of the bowl, tip out on to a lightly floured work surface and stretch it into a shape big enough to fit over the casserole and ham. Carefully lift it over the ham and stretch to the edges of the casserole. Pinch the dough all the way round to secure it to the casserole, except where the ham bone is (leave it loose around here, allowing the steam to escape).

Place in the oven to bake for one hour until golden brown. To check the bread is cooked through, tap it lightly; it should sound hollow. Remove and allow to cool for 15 minutes before serving directly on to the table. Break the bread crust, lift the ham out and carve, then spoon out the vegetables.

I'm a sucker for a take-out but, at my house, not many deliver... which is a bonus for my waistline. In this chapter are dishes I love to cook at home, learnt from chefs who are masters at their craft.

spicy comforts

THAI CRAB RISOTTO WITH LEMON GRASS AND KAFFIR LIME

Coriander cress is a micro-herb, the first young shoots of the growing herbs. You can of course grow it yourself, cutting it when it just starts to sprout, but micro-herbs are now available in some supermarkets.

Don't use too much Thai curry paste, because the flavour gets stronger as you cook and you can't take it out.

Serves 3 – 4

1 crab shell, broken up

300ml chicken stock

1 lemon grass stalk, tough outer layers removed, finely chopped

2 kaffir lime leaves, shredded

1 long red chilli, deseeded and roughly chopped

1 garlic clove

2 shallots

1 tbsp tomato purée

300ml vegetable oil

50g unsalted butter

75g arborio rice

1 tsp Thai green curry paste

75ml muscat wine

50ml double cream

50g picked brown crab meat

110g picked white crab meat

2 tbsp grated parmesan

1 tbsp mascarpone

1 green chilli, deseeded and finely chopped

1 tbsp roughly chopped coriander leaves

juice of 1 lime

sea salt and freshly ground black pepper

1 tbsp coriander cress (optional)

Preheat the oven to 200°C/400°F/gas mark 6.

Place half the crab shell into a saucepan with the chicken stock, lemon grass and one of the kaffir lime leaves and heat through.

Place the rest of the crab shell into a deep oven dish, then add the chilli and garlic, roughly chop one of the shallots and add it with the tomato purée. Pour over all the vegetable oil then place in the oven for 30 minutes until the shell is roasted. Mix well, then carefully strain the oil into a sterilised jar (see page 21) and set aside.

Heat a sauté pan until medium hot, then add the butter. Finely chop the remaining shallot and add along with the last kaffir lime leaf. Tip in the rice and stir well to coat in the buttery mix, then add the Thai green curry paste and wine and cook until nearly dry.

Add a couple of ladlefuls of crab stock at a time, simmering and stirring until the rice has absorbed all the stock, then add some more and continue to cook. Repeat until all the stock has been used and the rice is tender; it should take 15–18 minutes.

When the rice is tender, stir in the cream and fold in the picked crab. Add the parmesan, mascarpone, green chilli and coriander and finish with the lime juice, then check the seasoning.

Spoon on to a plate, then scatter with a little of the coriander cress (if using) and finish with a drizzle of the roasted, spiced crab oil from the jar.

SMOKY CHILLI CHICKEN WINGS, SPICED POTATO WEDGES AND PADRÓN PEPPERS

A Spanish friend of mine taught me this. It's so simple too but, as he stresses, you must use the correct vinegar and paprika or it won't work. Padrón peppers are like Russian roulette; about one in 10 are hot, so have a cold beer to hand in case it's you that gets it.

Serves 4 – 6

For the wedges

1 tsp Szechuan peppercorns, ground
1 tbsp ground coriander
1 tbsp ground cumin
1 tbsp sweet smoked paprika
3 tbsp olive oil
1 tsp sea salt
4 large potatoes, scrubbed and cut into wedges

For the chicken wings and peppers

12 large, meaty chicken wings
sea salt and freshly ground black pepper
3 tbsp olive oil, plus more for the chicken
6 tbsp extra virgin olive oil
6 garlic cloves, finely sliced
2 tsp hot smoked paprika
2 tbsp sherry vinegar
juice of ½ lemon, or to taste
150g padrón peppers

Preheat the oven to 220°C/425°F/gas mark 7.

For the wedges, mix the spices together in a bowl with the olive oil and salt, then add the potatoes and toss well to coat thoroughly.

Pour out on to a flat baking sheet and place in the oven for 25 minutes, turning halfway through, until they are golden, crunchy around the edges but tender when pierced with a knife.

Meanwhile, place the wings on a roasting tray, toss with salt, pepper and a little of the regular oil, then roast for 15–20 minutes until golden and cooked through.

Make the dressing: heat a frying pan until hot, add the virgin oil and garlic and cook for a couple of minutes over a gentle heat – you don't want to burn the garlic – then add the paprika and vinegar with a squeeze of lemon juice. Set aside.

When the wedges and wings are nearly ready, heat a frying pan until hot, add the 3 tbsp of regular oil and the peppers, then fry for two or three minutes until they are charred. Sprinkle with salt. Pile into a serving bowl and top with some more sea salt.

Put the wings in a serving bowl and drizzle with some of the warm garlic dressing. Serve with the wedges and padrón peppers.

You can deep-fry the peppers if you prefer, in good olive oil not vegetable oil, as you want the taste.

CHICKEN TAGINE WITH POMEGRANATE TABBOULEH

I know the ingredients list may be long, but the end result will be worth it all. The spices are so important, as is the mix of fruit in this dish. Tabbouleh can't have enough stuff added to it as far as I'm concerned; you need to pack it in to make it taste good. You can make the tabbouleh with couscous, but I think it's better with bulgar.

Serves 3 – 6

For the tagine

2 tbsp olive oil
6 large skin-on bone-in chicken thighs
1 onion, finely chopped
2 garlic cloves, finely chopped
5cm piece of root ginger, grated
½ tsp saffron strands
1 tsp turmeric
1 tsp ground coriander
1 tbsp ras el hanout
½ long cinnamon stick
500ml chicken stock
1 red chilli, finely sliced
2 tomatoes, roughly chopped
2 tbsp runny honey
2 tbsp roughly chopped mint leaves
2 tbsp roughly chopped coriander leaves
25g unsalted butter
sea salt and freshly ground black pepper

For the tabbouleh

150g bulgar wheat, soaked in water overnight
3 tbsp roughly chopped mint leaves
3 tbsp roughly chopped coriander leaves
½ red onion, finely chopped
50g pistachio nuts, roughly chopped
100g whole blanched almonds
100g dried apricots, roughly chopped
seeds from 1 pomegranate
juice of 2 lemons

Start with the tagine. Heat a large, heavy-based saucepan until hot, add the olive oil and chicken thighs skin side down and fry until golden brown, then flip over and seal on the other side before removing to a plate.

Add the onion, garlic and ginger to the pan and sweat for two or three minutes. Add all the ground spices and the cinnamon stick and cook for one minute, then return the chicken to the pan and stir well to coat.

Add the stock, chilli, tomatoes and honey and bring to the boil. Reduce the heat to a simmer, cover and cook for 20 minutes until the chicken is cooked through. Add the herbs, whisk in the butter, then check the seasoning.

Meanwhile, make the tabbouleh. Drain the bulgar wheat well, pressing down lightly to ensure all the water is removed, then place into a large bowl. Add all the other ingredients and mix well, then check the seasoning.

Pile the tabbouleh on plates and serve with the chicken and some sauce.

THAI LAMB SALAD WITH SPICY DRESSING

I love this dish. Frying the cold lamb until crisp on the edges gives it a great texture, then adding the brilliant dressing means you get masses of flavours in. You really need all the dressing ingredients sadly; it won't work with normal sugar or without the fish sauce. It doesn't need poncing around, just whack it on the plate and put it on the table. Simple. This is one of the dishes I do all the time at home.

Serves 4

2 red chillies, 1 chopped, 1 finely sliced

4 garlic cloves, crushed

90g root ginger, peeled and roughly chopped

2 tbsp palm sugar

6 tbsp soy sauce

4 tbsp fish sauce

300g cooked lamb, cut into thick slices, with the fat left on

½ cucumber, halved lengthways, sliced thinly on the diagonal

100g fresh podded peas, some in the pods if really fresh

100g sugar snap peas, sliced lengthways

75g beansprouts

6 spring onions, sliced on the diagonal

3 tbsp roughly chopped mint leaves

small handful of coriander sprigs

juice of 2 limes

25g pea shoots

Place the chopped chilli, the garlic, ginger and palm sugar into a food processor or mortar and pestle and blitz or grind to a fine paste. Add the soy and fish sauce then blitz once more. Taste and adjust if necessary.

Heat a frying pan until hot, add the fatty lamb and fry for two or three minutes until crispy on one side. Add half the dressing and heat through until sticky and coating the lamb nicely, then remove from the heat and set aside.

Place the cucumber, peas, sugar snaps, beansprouts, spring onions, mint and coriander into a bowl and toss to combine. Add some dressing and lime juice to the bowl then add the pea shoots and toss once more.

Divide the salad between the plates then top with the crispy lamb. Finish with more of the dressing, sprinkle on the finely sliced chilli and serve straight away.

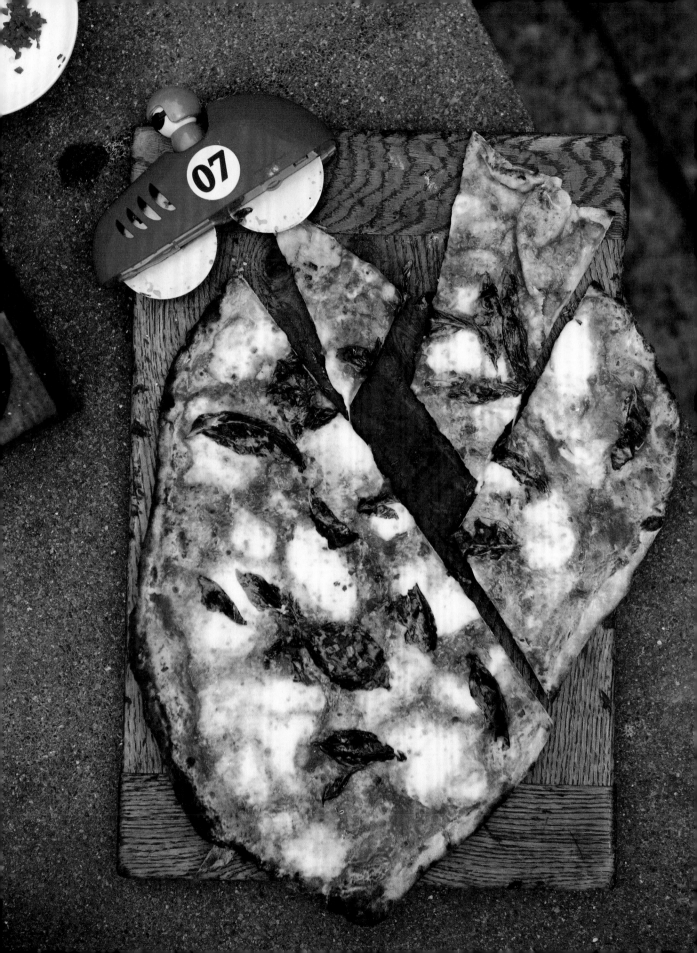

CHILLI TOMATO PIZZA AND LOBSTER CALZONE

Lobster pizza is a bit flash but you can make this with crab or prawns, or even with salmon. Whatever you use, make sure the fish filling is cooked beforehand as the pizza cooks so quickly that there is no time to cook the filling. The semolina flour will give both the pizza and the calzone a nice crust.

For best results, you need a pizza stone in your oven; and get the oven as hot as possible.

Serves 4–6

For the pizza dough

800g '00' flour, plus more to dust
200g semolina flour
1 tsp salt
1 tbsp caster sugar
2 x 7g sachets fast-action yeast

For the topping

2 x 400g cans of San Marzano tomatoes
2 large balls of cow's milk mozzarella, roughly torn
50g finely grated pecorino cheese
2 chillies, deseeded and finely sliced
4 tbsp peanut oil
large handful of basil leaves
sea salt and freshly ground black pepper
1 small cooked lobster
bottle of mango chilli sauce

To make the dough, place the flour, semolina, salt, sugar and yeast into a large bowl and stir. Make a well in the centre of the flour and pour in 650ml of water, gradually mixing with the flour to form a soft dough.

Tip out and knead on a lightly floured work surface until smooth and elastic. Divide into four and roll each into a ball, then place on a tray, cover and leave to rise for 24 hours.

Preheat the oven to as high as it will go. Place a heavy baking tray or pizza stone in the oven and allow to heat.

Roll each piece of dough out until about 5mm thick, then place on to an upturned floured tray.

Make the topping. Place the tomatoes in a food processor and blitz to a purée. Spoon thinly over two of the pizzas, just to the edges.

Scatter over half the mozzarella and pecorino and all the chillies, then drizzle over half the peanut oil. Finish with a few basil leaves and season with salt and black pepper.

Scoot into the oven – pushing the pizza from the tray on to the heated tray or pizza stone – and cook for five to eight minutes until cooked through and bubbling. Serve immediately.

Meanwhile, cover half of each of the other pizzas with the tomato sauce, then place pieces of lobster over that half, with the remaining mozzarella, pecorino, a drizzle of mango chilli sauce, the remaining peanut oil and a scattering of basil. Season with salt and pepper.

Fold the empty halves of the pizzas over the filled halves, then crimp the edges and place on the heated pizza tray or stone.

Cook for five to 10 minutes until golden and crispy. Serve immediately.

INDIAN-SPICED LAMB SHOULDER WITH BOMBAY POTATOES

Lots of my mates are Indian and I've learned a few tips from them over the years. I have had to, as they've come for dinner a few times! This is my go-to recipe: you just stick it in the oven and forget about it. Using a lamb shoulder means you have to cook it for a while, but the taste will be worth it in the end.

Serves 4–6

For the spice mix

1 tbsp coriander seeds

1½ tsp each cumin seeds, chilli flakes and turmeric

1 cinnamon stick, broken up

½ tsp each fennel seeds, peppercorns and fenugreek

¼ tsp cloves

For the lamb

1 lamb shoulder

sea salt and freshly ground black pepper

2 tbsp vegetable oil

2 onions, finely chopped

2 green finger chillies, split lengthways

4 garlic cloves, finely chopped

5cm piece of root ginger, finely chopped

1 tsp cardamom pods, lightly crushed

8 curry leaves

2 tbsp tamarind pulp

400g can of chopped tomatoes

1 litre beef stock

2 tbsp chopped coriander leaves

2 tbsp chopped mint leaves

For the Bombay potatoes

750g potatoes, cut into 3cm cubes

4 tbsp flavourless vegetable oil

1 onion, finely chopped

1 garlic clove, finely chopped

1 tsp each mustard seeds, chilli powder, ground coriander and cumin

½ tsp turmeric

400g can of chopped tomatoes

1 tbsp each chopped coriander and mint leaves

To make the spice mix, place the coriander and cumin seeds into a dry frying pan and heat for one or two minutes until just browning and aromatic. Pour into a spice grinder or a mortar and pestle with the rest of the spices and blitz to a powder.

For the lamb, preheat the oven to 150°C/300°F/gas mark 2. Season the lamb with plenty of salt and pepper. Heat the vegetable oil in a large non-stick casserole pan and sear the lamb for two minutes on each side until golden-brown all over, then remove from the pan and set aside.

Add the onions and chillies and cook for four or five minutes until softened and just coloured. Add the spice mix, garlic and ginger, mix well and cook for another two minutes, then add the cardamom, curry leaves and tamarind.

Add the chopped tomatoes and stock and bring to the boil, then reduce the heat to a simmer and cover. Cook in the oven for three to four hours, until the lamb is virtually falling off the bone. Remove the lid, baste the lamb with the sauce and cook for another five minutes. Season to taste with salt and black pepper, then stir in the herbs.

Meanwhile, make the Bombay potatoes. Place the potatoes in cold water, bring to the boil and cook for 12–15 minutes, then drain.

Heat a large sauté pan and add the oil. Once it is hot, add the onion, garlic, mustard seeds, chilli powder, ground coriander and cumin and turmeric. Tip in the tomatoes, mix really well and bring to a gentle simmer, then add the potatoes and cook for another three to five minutes until they absorb the spices and are very tender. Season to taste, then stir in the herbs.

Pile chunks of the lamb carefully on to each plate, then spoon the sauce over and serve with a pile of potatoes.

CHILLI BEEF RENDANG

Indonesia and Malaysia are the main parts of the world where this spicy dish comes from and the mixture of spices is something I picked up from a great place I visited in Singapore. And it seems it's one dish that us Brits love. The main flavour here comes from coconut and cooking it slow really makes the dish shine.

Serves 4

2 large banana shallots, roughly chopped

5cm piece of root ginger, peeled and roughly chopped

2 lemon grass stalks, tough outer layers discarded, roughly chopped

3 kaffir lime leaves, roughly chopped

6 garlic cloves, roughly chopped

4 long red chillies, roughly chopped

1kg stewing beef, cut into cubes

1–2 small dried chillies, depending on how hot you like it

1 tbsp rapeseed oil

5 cardamom pods, lightly crushed

3 star anise

2 cinnamon sticks

1 tbsp ground cumin

1 tbsp ground coriander

400ml can of coconut milk

200ml beef stock

1 tbsp fish sauce

1 tbsp palm sugar

2 tbsp tamarind paste

sea salt and freshly ground black pepper

juice of 2 limes

boiled jasmine rice, to serve

Put the shallots, ginger, lemon grass, lime leaves, garlic, red chillies and 5 tbsp of water into a food processor and blitz to form a paste, then scoop it out into a large bowl and add the beef. Stir well to coat. Cover and set aside to marinate for at least two hours, preferably overnight in the fridge.

When ready to cook, put the dried chillies into a bowl and cover with hot water from the kettle. Set aside for 30 minutes to soften.

Heat a casserole over a medium heat with the rapeseed oil. Add the cardamom, star anise, cinnamon, cumin and coriander and toast for a few seconds until aromatic, then add the marinated beef. Stir well. Add all the remaining ingredients except the lime juice and bring to a simmer.

Drain the dried chillies – reserving the water – and finely chop them, then add them and 50ml of their soaking water to the pan and stir well. Cover with a lid and simmer for two hours until the beef is tender.

Remove the lid and stir well, then cook for another 15–20 minutes until the sauce is thickened and coating the beef. Add the lime juice and season to taste with salt and pepper.

Serve with jasmine rice.

INDIAN SOFT SHELL CRABS
WITH HOME-MADE LIME PICKLE

Soft shell crabs will more often than not be bought frozen; they can be found online or from good fishmongers. So buy plenty at a time, as you can keep them in the freezer at home. You need hot oil to fry them and you'll need an oil thermometer to get the right temperature; don't guess for this as you need to get the inside cooked and the outside nice and crisp to get the contrasting textures right.

Serves 4 as a starter

For the lime pickle

500g limes, cut into wedges
2 tbsp fine sea salt
1 tbsp vegetable oil
1 tbsp mustard seeds
4 garlic cloves, finely chopped
5cm piece of root ginger, peeled and finely chopped
1 tbsp ground cumin
1 tbsp ground coriander
½ tsp asafoetida
1½ tsp mild chilli powder
300g soft light brown sugar
50ml white wine vinegar

For the crab

5cm piece of root ginger, peeled and grated
4 garlic cloves, crushed
1 tbsp ground coriander
2 tsp ground cumin
1 tsp chilli powder
4 tbsp chopped coriander leaves and roots
4 tbsp gram flour
finely grated zest and juice of 2 limes
4 tbsp groundnut oil
8 small soft shell crabs
flavourless vegetable oil, to deep-fry

First, make the lime pickle; it's best to make it a week or so before. Place the limes and salt into a bowl and toss to combine, then cover and place in the fridge to cure for 48 hours, stirring occasionally.

Heat a large sauté pan over a high heat, then add the oil and mustard seeds. As soon as they start popping, add the garlic and ginger and stir for one minute. Add the cumin, coriander, asafoetida and chilli powder and stir for another minute, then add the sugar and cook, without stirring, until it liquefies, shaking the pan occasionally. Now tip in the salted limes and the juices from the bowl, the vinegar and 200ml of water.

Bring to the boil, then reduce the heat, cover and simmer for 1½ hours over a gentle heat, until thickened and the limes are very soft. Cool slightly before pulsing in a food processor for 20 seconds until the pieces of lime are quite small. Spoon into sterilised jars (see page 21) and ideally leave for a few days to mature.

For the crab, place all the ingredients except the crabs and the oil for deep-frying into a bowl and mix to a thick paste, then add the crabs and mix well so the crabs are coated in the mixture.

Cover and place in the fridge for at least two hours. Remove from the fridge and bring to room temperature before you want to cook them.

Heat a deep fat fryer to 160°C/320°F or heat the oil for deep-frying in a deep heavy-based sauté pan until a breadcrumb sizzles and turns brown when dropped into it. (CAUTION: hot oil can be dangerous. Do not leave unattended.)

Carefully lay the crabs one at a time into the oil and cook for one or two minutes until cooked through. Drain on kitchen paper and season with a little salt.

Serve the crabs with generous dollops of lime pickle.

LEMON GRASS AND GINGER MUSSELS

It used to be that you were advised to only buy mussels when there was an 'r' in the month. I never really knew where that came from, as I've been to loads of farms around the country producing mussels all year round, they're cheap and packed full of flavour. Stuff such as lemon grass and ginger are commonplace in supermarkets nowadays and the flavours here with the coconut make it really tasty. Try not to reduce the liquid too much, as you will want to mop up the liquor left in the bowl with plenty of bread. Add a squeeze of lime juice if you want it, too.

Serves 4

2kg mussels, scrubbed, beards removed

50g unsalted butter

2 shallots, finely chopped

2 lemon grass stalks, outer layers discarded, finely chopped

2 garlic cloves, finely chopped

10cm piece of root ginger, peeled and finely chopped

1–2 red chillies (depending on their heat), finely sliced

200ml white wine

330ml coconut water

160ml coconut cream

2 tbsp olive oil

1 loaf sourdough bread, thickly sliced

2 tbsp roughly chopped coriander leaves

Wash the mussels in a colander to remove any dirt or grit and discard any of the beards (the tufty bits on the mussels). If you want to be fussy, scrape off any little barnacles with an old butter knife, too. Throw away any mussels that are not firmly closed, and don't shut when tapped firmly on the side of the sink.

Place the butter in a large pan and, when it's foaming, add the shallots, lemon grass, garlic, ginger and chilli(es) and cook without colour for five minutes until soft.

Increase the heat to high and add the wine, coconut water and coconut cream, bring to the boil, then add the mussels. Cover and cook for four to five minutes until the mussels open.

Meanwhile, heat a griddle pan until hot. Drizzle the olive oil over the bread and char on each side until golden.

Add the coriander leaves to the mussels and stir through, then check the seasoning.

Serve the mussels with the charred bread, discarding any shellfish that have refused to open and warning your guests to do the same.

LEBANESE SPICED
LAMB FLATBREAD

*This is a recipe I've tweaked: it was for chunks of lamb, but
I changed it to mince to speed it up. Instead of bread
I've used a pizza base, as I love my pizza oven in the garden.
You can buy a pizza stone for your regular oven and heat it
with the oven on full whack and you get a similar effect.*

Serves 8

For the pizza dough

400g '00' flour, plus more to dust
100g semolina flour
½ tsp salt
1½ tsp caster sugar
7g sachet of fast-action yeast
325ml warm water

For the filling

1 tbsp vegetable oil
1 shallot, finely chopped
1 garlic clove, finely chopped
1 tsp ground coriander
1 tsp ground cumin
1 tbsp ground baharat spice mix
500g minced lamb
75g sultanas
300ml chicken stock
sea salt and freshly ground black pepper
250ml natural yogurt
2 green chillies, finely chopped
leaves from 4 sprigs of mint
leaves from 16 sprigs of coriander

Start the day before by making the dough. Place the flours, salt and sugar into a large bowl and stir. Mix the yeast with a little of the water in a jug to form a paste, then add the rest of the water to the jug, so that the yeast is dissolved into the water.

Make a well in the centre of the flour and pour the yeasted water, gradually mixing to form a soft dough.

Tip out and knead on a lightly floured work surface until smooth and elastic.

Divide into four and roll each into a ball, then place on a tray, cover and leave to rise for 24 hours.

For the filling, heat a sauté pan until hot, add the oil, shallot, garlic and spices and cook for two minutes, then add the lamb and cook over a high heat, turning frequently and breaking up with the spoon, until browned.

Add the sultanas and chicken stock and bring to the boil, then reduce the heat and simmer for 20 minutes until the lamb is tender and the liquid virtually gone. Season to taste, then allow to cool totally.

Preheat the oven to as high as it will go. Place a heavy baking tray or pizza stone in the oven and allow to heat.

Roll each piece of dough out on a lightly floured surface into an oval roughly 20 x 15cm, and about 5mm thick, then place on to an upturned, floured baking tray.

Cover the dough bases with the lamb mixture, then evenly scatter over the yogurt and chillies and season with salt and pepper.

Place on the heated tray or stone (you may have to cook them in batches) and cook for five to 10 minutes until golden and crispy. Scatter with the herbs and serve immediately.

SWEET-AND-SOUR PORK AND PINEAPPLE WITH EGG-FRIED RICE

All the components here are simple, but it requires back-timing so everything is ready at the same time. The solution is this: don't be afraid to ask for help in the kitchen. Ken Hom showed me this one and it's fantastic. He really is the master at this stuff. Enjoy it! The usual warnings about using cold cooked rice apply (see page 42). If you prefer, you can pair it with a Sticky rice omelette (see overleaf) instead of egg-fried rice.

Serves 4

For the pork

450g pork fillet, cut into 5cm-long strips

2 tsp light soy sauce

2 tsp Shaoxing rice wine or dry sherry

1 tsp sesame oil

2 tsp cornflour

1½ tbsp groundnut oil

3 tbsp coarsely chopped garlic

225g fresh or canned pineapple, chopped

2 tbsp finely chopped coriander leaves, plus a large handful of sprigs of coriander

1 tbsp dark soy sauce

2 tsp caster sugar

For the egg-fried rice

2 eggs, lightly beaten

2 tsp sesame oil

1 tsp salt

2 tbsp groundnut or vegetable oil

400g long-grain rice, cooked, drained and chilled

½ tsp freshly ground black pepper

2 tbsp spring onions, finely chopped

Put the pork in a bowl with the light soy sauce, rice wine or sherry, sesame oil and cornflour and set aside.

Heat a wok over high heat until it is hot, add the oil and, when it is very hot and slightly smoking, add the garlic and stir-fry for 15 seconds or until golden brown. Then add the pork and stir-fry for three minutes.

Add the pineapple, coriander leaves, dark soy sauce and sugar and continue to stir-fry for another three minutes. Spoon on to a platter and garnish with the sprigs of coriander.

Meanwhile, to cook the egg-fried rice, mix the eggs, sesame oil and a pinch of the salt in a small bowl and set aside.

Heat a wok or large frying pan over high heat until it is hot. Add the groundnut or vegetable oil and, when it is very hot and slightly smoking, add the cooked rice and stir-fry for three minutes or until it is thoroughly warmed through.

Drizzle the egg mixture over the rice and continue to stir-fry for two or three minutes or until the eggs have set and the mixture is dry. Add the remaining salt and the pepper, stir-fry for two more minutes, then toss in the spring onions. Stir several times and turn on to a serving plate.

TEMPURA SQUID AND PRAWNS WITH ASIAN 'PESTO'

This 'pesto' has tonnes of flavour and works well with most meat and fish. I love squid now. If I'm honest I never used to but, like most things, it's wasted on the young! Fry the squid in oil that is as hot as you dare, as you don't want it to overcook.

Serves 4

For the tempura

flavourless vegetable oil, to deep-fry
500g squid, cleaned and cut into strips
500g raw king prawns, shelled and deveined
2 tbsp light soy sauce
2 tbsp Shaoxing rice wine or dry sherry
2 tbsp sesame oil
2 limes
100g cornflour
3 spring onions, finely sliced
1 long red chilli, roughly chopped

For the pesto

small handful of coriander leaves, roughly chopped
small handful of mint leaves, roughly chopped
1 garlic clove, sliced
1 long red chilli, sliced
2 tbsp palm sugar
1 tbsp fish sauce
1 tbsp soy sauce
1 tbsp sesame oil
1 tbsp Shaoxing rice wine or dry sherry
juice of 1 lime

Heat a deep-fat fryer to 180°C/350°F, or heat the oil for deep-frying in a deep heavy-based saucepan until a breadcrumb sizzles and turns brown when dropped into it. (CAUTION: hot oil can be dangerous. Do not leave unattended.)

While it heats up, put the squid and prawns into a bowl and mix them with the soy sauce, rice wine or sherry, sesame oil and the juice of 1 lime.

To make the pesto, put half the herbs and all the other ingredients into a small food processor and blitz well to make a fine purée.

Add the cornflour to the squid and prawns and mix well to coat; it will be very sticky.

Carefully place the seafood into the fat fryer in batches and fry for two minutes, until just cooked through and crispy. Drain on kitchen paper to blot off excess fat while you quickly cook the rest.

Lay the cooked seafood on a platter then drizzle over the pesto, scatter over the reserved herbs and finish with the spring onions and chopped chilli.

Cut the remaining lime into wedges and place alongside.

CHILLI BEEF WITH A STICKY RICE OMELETTE

Make sure you reduce the sauce for the beef down until sticky, as you want the meat to be coated in the sauce. The usual warnings about using cold cooked rice apply (see page 42).

Serves 3 – 4

For the chilli beef

flavourless vegetable oil, to deep-fry, plus 2 tbsp

400g beef fillet, cut into thin strips

1 tbsp Szechuan peppercorns

finely grated zest of 2 limes

finely grated zest of 1 orange

3 heaped tbsp rice flour, potato flour or cornflour

For the sauce

150g caster sugar

150ml Shaoxing rice wine

25ml rice wine vinegar

2 tbsp soy sauce

1½ red chillies, deseeded and finely chopped

2 tsp chilli flakes

10cm root ginger, peeled and finely chopped

2 lemon grass stalks, outer leaves removed, finely chopped

4 lime leaves, finely chopped

For the sticky rice omelette

1 tbsp vegetable oil

4 eggs

2 tbsp soy sauce

400g sticky rice, cooked and drained, at room temperature

Heat a deep-fat fryer to 190°C/375°F or heat the oil for deep-frying in a deep heavy-based frying pan until a breadcrumb sizzles and turns brown when dropped into it. (CAUTION: hot oil can be dangerous. Do not leave unattended.)

Toss the beef strips with the 2 tbsp of vegetable oil.

Place the Szechuan peppercorns into a mortar and pestle and crush to a fine powder. Place them in large bowl with the lime and orange zests and rice flour, then toss well to combine. Add the beef and toss to coat each piece.

Drop a small batch of the beef into the fat fryer and cook for two minutes. Don't overcrowd the pan. Drain on kitchen paper to blot off the excess fat. Keep warm while you cook the rest.

Now make the sauce. Heat a frying pan or wok until hot, add the sugar, rice wine, vinegar and soy sauce and bring to the boil. Add the chillies, chilli flakes, ginger, lemon grass and lime leaves, then cook for five to eight minutes until thickened, sticky and glossy looking.

Add the cooked beef to the sauce, remove from the heat and toss well so that all the beef is coated in sticky chilli sauce.

Now for the omelette. Heat a wok until hot, add the oil and swirl to coat before very carefully wiping the wok out with kitchen towel, removing any excess oil.

Whisk the eggs together with the soy sauce then pour into the hot wok, lifting the wok up and rolling the egg around the sides of it so you have one very large omelette.

Add the cooked rice to the centre of the omelette then carefully peel the omelette away from the sides of the wok to cover the rice.

When the rice is hot through and the omelette set, roll out on to a board and cut into four.

Pile the beef on to a plate or into bowls and serve the rice omelette on a board alongside.

Anyone who knows me will know I have a sweet tooth. I was put on the pastry section while training as a chef. I loved it, even though you're the first to start and the last to leave. Here is a small cross-section of those years of 18-hour days. From the amazing three Michelin star lemon tart from a London restaurant to the best-ever chocolate truffles.

sweet comforts

STRAWBERRY AND WHITE CHOCOLATE CHEESECAKE

As a keen gardener, there are few things I look forward to more in my garden than fresh strawberries: the one ingredient that, to me, signals that summer is here. When you have fruit this good, cooking it would be a waste. Sure the glaze is cooked, but it's only a small part of the dish and it's delicious. The cheesecake is so simple and quick and, in this recipe, using a sponge base tastes better than biscuit.

Serves 6–8

200g white chocolate, roughly chopped
750g strawberries, hulled and halved
100g caster sugar
2 sheets of gelatine, soaked in cold water
1 large sponge flan case
2–3 tbsp fruit liqueur, brandy or whisky (optional)
200g full-fat cream cheese
200ml crème fraîche
325ml double cream
1 vanilla pod, split, seeds scraped out

Melt the white chocolate in a bowl set over a pan of simmering water (the bowl should not touch the water). When totally melted, pour on to a large baking sheet lined with greaseproof paper and tip from side to side until it covers the tray in a layer about 5mm thick. Place in the freezer for about 10–20 minutes until frozen.

Place 300g of the strawberries into a saucepan with 25g of the caster sugar and 75ml of water and bring to the boil. Reduce the heat and simmer for three to four minutes.

Pass through a fine sieve into a bowl, then add the soaked gelatine – squeezing out any excess liquid – and stir until totally dissolved. Allow to cool to room temperature.

Use a 20–25cm stainless steel ring to cut out the centre of the flan case. We used a triangle mould for the photo because we were feeling poncey. With a sharp knife, cut the sponge in half horizontally so you end up with two thin pieces. Set one half on a serving plate and save the other half for another time, or blitz for cake crumbs. Place the ring back over the sponge disc, then drizzle over the fruit liqueur (if using).

Put the cream cheese, crème fraîche, double cream, remaining sugar and vanilla seeds into a bowl and whisk until well combined.

Spoon the cheese mixture into the ring, making sure that it is pressed into the edges. Smooth the top with a palette knife.

Cover the top of the cheesecake with the rest of the strawberries, then lift the ring off (warming quickly with a blowtorch is the best way to remove the ring cleanly; if you haven't got one, dip a cloth into hot water and run around the ring).

Drizzle over the strawberry glaze.

Break the frozen white chocolate into shards and press around the edge of the cheesecake until totally covered.

Serve straight away.

PASSION FRUIT CRÈME WITH COCONUT AND CHERRY BISCOTTI

I love this. For me, the flavour of passion fruit gives so much bang for its buck. Baking your own biscotti is something you will do again and again once you taste them. And they are so simple with this recipe.

Serves 4

For the passion fruit crème
600ml double cream
250g caster sugar
juice of 1 lime
150ml passion fruit pulp (passed through a fine sieve)
2 leaves of gelatine

For the biscotti
300g plain flour, plus more to dust
250g caster sugar
100g shelled pistachios
60g grated fresh coconut
50g natural glacé cherries, roughly chopped
finely grated zest and juice of 1 unwaxed lemon
1¼ tsp baking powder
pinch of salt
3 eggs, lightly beaten

Begin with the passion fruit crème. Put the double cream and 150g of the sugar into a large saucepan. Gently bring to the boil, then remove from the heat. Add the lime juice and 75ml of the passion fruit pulp and whisk to combine.

Pour into four large martini glasses and place in the fridge to set for at least two hours.

Meanwhile, soak the gelatine leaves in cold water. Put the remaining 100g of caster sugar into a saucepan with 100ml of water, bring to the boil, then squeeze any excess water out of the gelatine, add to the syrup and whisk until completely dissolved. Add the remaining 75ml passion fruit pulp, then set aside to cool.

When it's cool, pour over the passion fruit crème to cover (this layer only needs to be about 5mm thick). Return to the fridge to set for another hour. Remove from the fridge for 30 minutes before serving.

Meanwhile, make the biscotti, Preheat the oven to 180°C/350°F/gas mark 4 and line a baking tray with a layer of baking parchment.

Mix all the ingredients in a bowl and mix together to a soft, sticky dough. Form it into two long sausages on a lightly floured work surface, place on the baking tray, then bake in the oven for 20–30 minutes until golden brown.

Remove from the oven and leave for 10 minutes to cool and firm up.

Using a serrated knife, cut the biscotti on an angle into slices 1cm thick, then lay them back on to the baking tray (you may well need two trays now).

Return to the oven and cook for eight minutes, then turn the slices over and cook for a further 10–15 minutes or until a pale golden colour on both sides. Remove from the oven and cool on wire racks.

Serve the passion fruit crème with the biscotti alongside.

You can use oranges for this, too. Make sure you pat the sliced fruit dry slightly before using it to line the dish.

STEAMED CHOCOLATE AND CLEMENTINE SPONGE WITH ORANGE SAUCE

You can make this with oranges if you wish, but it is definitely a winter pudding. At Christmas, we all seem to have a glut of clementines left over after the frantic stocking up for the festive period. This is an excellent way to use them up and a great rib-sticking pud to indulge yourself with in the cold weather.

Serves 4 – 6

For the sponge

175g unsalted butter, softened, plus more for the bowl
8 clementines
175g golden caster sugar
3 medium eggs, lightly beaten
125g self-raising flour
50g cocoa powder
1 tsp baking powder
pinch of salt

For the orange sauce

75g caster sugar
½ vanilla pod, split, seeds scraped out
50ml orange liqueur
100ml orange juice
juice of 1 clementine
40g unsalted butter
200g crème fraîche

Start with the sponge. Butter a 1.2-litre heatproof bowl. Carefully cut the skin from the clementines and cut into thick slices. Pat dry, then lay the clementine slices into the buttered bowl, one in the centre then five around it, repeating all the way up the side of the bowl.

Place the butter, sugar, eggs, flour, cocoa, baking powder and salt into a bowl and whisk until light and fluffy. Spoon carefully into the clementine-lined bowl.

Lay a sheet of greaseproof paper on to a sheet of foil, pleat both layers in the centre to create an overlap, then tie around the bowl with string. Take a long piece of foil and fold lengthways in half to make a handle.

Place a cloth in the base of a large saucepan, then put an upside-down saucer or small plate on it. Fill halfway up with water. Place the foil-covered bowl on to the long folded over piece of foil, then into the saucepan (this acts as a handle later to lift the pudding bowl out of the saucepan). Cover and bring to a boil, then reduce the heat and simmer for 1½–2 hours.

For the sauce, heat a sauté pan until hot, add the caster sugar and vanilla seeds and heat, without stirring, until it turns to a light golden caramel, shaking the pan from time to time. Add the orange liqueur and, standing well back, set alight. When the flames die down, add the orange and clementine juices and cook for two or three minutes until it comes together into a thin sauce. Add the butter and swirl to combine and thicken.

Use the foil strip to lift the pudding bowl out of the saucepan, then discard the foil and baking parchment. Place a plate on top and turn over, tipping the pudding on to the plate. Pour the sauce over the top, offer some crème fraîche on the side, then dig in!

RASPBERRY, WHITE CHOCOLATE AND CARAMEL PAVLOVA

Look at the picture. Just look at it. If that doesn't tempt you to make this, I don't know what will.

Serves 6 – 8

6 egg whites

500g caster sugar

1 tbsp cornflour

1 tbsp white wine vinegar

200g white chocolate, roughly chopped

500ml double cream

200ml ready-made vanilla custard

2–3 punnets of raspberries, depending how generous you are feeling

lemon verbena leaves, or mint leaves, to serve

Preheat the oven to 150°C/300°F/gas mark 2. Line a large baking tray with baking parchment.

Whisk the egg whites with an electric whisk on high speed and add 300g of the sugar a spoonful at a time, whisking until smooth and glossy. Reduce the speed of the whisk and add the cornflour and vinegar. Return the whisk to high speed and whisk until the mixture is stiff.

Spread with a spatula – or pipe it, if you prefer – into a round on the prepared tray and place in the oven for two or three hours. Now turn off the oven and leave the pavlova in there for six to eight hours or overnight to dry out, then place on a serving plate.

Melt the white chocolate in a heatproof bowl over a pan of simmering (not boiling) water. The bowl should not touch the water. Brush the white chocolate over the meringue and allow to cool.

Whisk the cream until soft peaks form, then whisk in the custard until at the soft peaks stage once more. Spread the cream over the cooled chocolate.

Heat the remaining 200g caster sugar in a saucepan over a medium heat until liquid and golden. Don't stir it, but swirl the pan from time to time.

Arrange the raspberries on the cream, then drizzle the caramel over the top. Sprinkle with lemon verbena or mint leaves, to serve.

RASPBERRY JELLY WITH LIME SYRUP AND HOME-MADE VANILLA ICE CREAM

Jelly and ice cream for grown ups! Of course you can leave out the vodka if you prefer, or if you are serving this to children.

Serves 8–10

For the jelly

450g caster sugar

8 gelatine leaves

50ml raspberry cordial, or raspberry and rose cordial

75–100ml vodka

flavourless vegetable oil, for the moulds

350g raspberries

For the ice cream

500ml whole milk

500ml double cream

1 vanilla pod, split, seeds scraped out

8 egg yolks

200g caster sugar

For the sauce

50ml lime cordial

1½ tsp arrowroot

finely grated zest of 3 limes

To make the jelly, put the sugar into a pan with 1 litre of water and bring to the boil. Meanwhile, soak the gelatine in a little cold water until softened. When the syrup has boiled, measure 1 litre of it into a jug (reserve the 200ml left over for the sauce), then squeeze the gelatine to remove any excess water. Add the gelatine to the measured syrup and mix gently to dissolve. Add the raspberry cordial and vodka and mix to combine.

Brush the inside of two 500g terrine moulds with the oil, then lay in cling film to cover it totally, with at least 2cm hanging over the edge. Place the moulds on a tray filled with ice.

Spoon enough jelly into the moulds to make a 1cm layer. Arrange the raspberries on the jelly, then cover with another layer of jelly. Allow this layer to partially set in the fridge for 30–45 minutes before adding more raspberries and jelly, reserving a few raspberries to serve (if the remaining jelly has set too much to pour, gently heat it to liquefy first). Place in the fridge for at least four hours to set.

For the ice cream, place the milk, cream and vanilla seeds into a saucepan and bring to the boil. Whisk the egg yolks and sugar in a bowl.

Pour the boiling cream mixture over the eggs, whisking all the time, then tip back into the saucepan, place over a high heat and cook, still whisking all the time, until the mixture thickens. Remove from the heat and pass through a fine sieve into a bowl to cool down. Once cool, transfer to an ice cream maker and churn until frozen.

Scoop into a lidded freezerproof container and freeze until needed.

To make the sauce, place the remaining 200ml sugar syrup into a pan with the lime cordial and bring to a simmer. Dissolve the arrowroot in a little cold water, then whisk it into the syrup and cook until it is thick enough to coat the back of a spoon. Remove from the heat, stir in the lime zest and allow to cool.

Turn the jelly out of the moulds and remove the cling film, then cut into slices. Serve with the reserved raspberries, some ice cream and a drizzle of the lime syrup.

WHITE CHOCOLATE AND WHISKY CROISSANT PUDDING WITH HONEYCOMB FOAM AND WHISKY ICE CREAM

My trademark dish, or so people tell me: bucket loads of butter, cream and calories. Just forget all that and enjoy it as it hasn't been off my restaurant menu in 22 years and is still one of the biggest sellers. Obviously, this is not for kids! You can buy lecithin in some supermarkets now, but also from health food shops and online.

Serves 6

For the whisky ice cream

100ml double cream
400ml whole milk
empty vanilla pod
6 egg yolks
100g caster sugar
100ml whisky

For the pudding

3 large all-butter croissants, thickly sliced
25g sultanas
40g unsalted butter, softened
500ml double cream
500ml whole milk
1 vanilla pod, split, seeds scraped out
300g white chocolate, roughly chopped
3 whole eggs, plus 6 egg yolks
200g caster sugar
75ml whisky
2 tbsp icing sugar, to dust

For the honeycomb foam

400ml whole milk
75g honeycomb, roughly chopped
  (for home-made, see page 167)
1 tsp lecithin powder

For the ice cream, put the cream and milk into a saucepan with the vanilla pod and bring to a simmer. Whisk the egg yolks and sugar together.

Add the whisky to the hot cream and return to a simmer, then pour over the eggs, whisking constantly to combine. Return to the pan and, whisking constantly, heat gently until thick enough to coat the back of a spoon.

Churn in an ice cream machine, then decant into a lidded freezerproof container and freeze until needed.

To make the pudding, lay the croissants into an ovenproof dish with the sultanas layered in between, then dot with the softened butter. Try to make sure no sultanas show on top, or they could burn.

Place the cream, milk and vanilla seeds into a saucepan and bring to the boil, then add the chocolate and whisk until totally melted.

Place the eggs, egg yolks and sugar into a bowl and whisk to combine.

Pour the hot chocolate custard through a sieve over the eggs (reserve the vanilla pod) and whisk to combine, pour in the whisky, then ladle it through a fine sieve over the croissant pudding and set aside for 20 minutes to soak. Preheat the oven to 180°C/350°F/gas mark 4.

Cover the pudding with foil and place in the oven for 25–30 minutes until golden and just set.

Remove from the oven and dust with the icing sugar. Place under a hot grill to caramelise, or use a blowtorch.

To create the foam, place the milk, honeycomb and lecithin into a small saucepan and heat until simmering, then froth with a stick blender until it is foaming.

Place a serving of the pudding into the centre of a plate, with some of the sauce from the dish, top with ice cream and add a spoonful of foam.

PEACH MELBA WITH SUGAR-ROASTED DOUGHNUTS

I learned to make real doughnuts at one of the oldest bake shops in the USA. They made all fancy shapes, but the biggest seller was the regular kind. Better still if you make small doughnuts like these, as you don't have to prove them for a second time, you can just fry them straight away.

Serves 4

For the doughnuts

250g strong white bread flour
pinch of salt
25g caster sugar, plus 75g to dust
25g unsalted butter, softened and chopped
2 x 7g sachets of fast-action yeast
flavourless vegetable oil, to deep-fry

For the rest

75g caster sugar
2 tbsp brandy
juice of 1 orange
200g canned sliced peaches
25g flaked almonds
25g pistachio nuts
100g raspberries
500g vanilla ice cream

To make the doughnuts, place the flour, salt, sugar and butter into a bowl. Put the yeast into a jug and mix with 150ml of water until smooth, then pour into the flour mixture.

Mix well, then knead to a smooth dough. Put in a bowl, cover and rest for one hour, until doubled in size.

When the dough has proved, heat the oil for deep-frying in a deep-fat fryer to 150°C/300°F. Alternatively, heat the oil in a deep, heavy-based saucepan until a breadcrumb sizzles and turns brown when dropped into it. (CAUTION: hot oil can be dangerous. Do not leave unattended.)

Take small golf ball-sized pieces of the dough and roll into balls.

Carefully lower the dough balls into the hot oil in batches and deep-fry for three or four minutes, or until golden-brown. Remove from the pan using a slotted spoon and set aside to drain on kitchen paper. Roll in the 75g of sugar.

For the sauce, heat a frying pan until hot, add the caster sugar and heat until it forms a caramel, swirling the pan occasionally (don't stir it).

Add the brandy, stand well back and set light to the pan then, when the flames subside, pour in the orange juice and swirl to combine.

Add the peaches, almonds, pistachio nuts and raspberries and heat through for two minutes only; you don't want to let the raspberries break down.

Place two spoonfuls of ice cream into each bowl, add a few doughnuts, then pour the sauce on top.

GÂTEAU ST HONORÉ

Named after the patron saint of pastry chefs, this should be on every menu around. I wish it was, anyway, but it's a bit of a fiddle to make and that's the reason it isn't.

Serves 8–10

For the choux pastry
125ml whole milk
100g unsalted butter, cut into small cubes
1 tsp caster sugar
175g plain flour
4 eggs

For the filling
300ml double cream
200ml vanilla custard (for home-made, see page 161)
50ml orange liqueur
100g caster sugar
200g mixed soft fruit, such as strawberries, raspberries, blackberries and currants
2 small twisted willow sprigs, to decorate (optional)

Preheat the oven to 200°C/400°F/gas mark 6. Line two baking sheets with silicone mats or paper.

Put the milk, 125ml of water, the butter and sugar into a saucepan and set over a high heat until the butter has melted (do not boil). Add the flour, beating well with a spatula and cook for one minute. Tip into a food mixer and beat for a couple of minutes to cool the mixture. Add the eggs, one at a time, beating well after each addition until the mixture is smooth.

Place into a piping bag and pipe a large Catherine wheel shape, about 24cm in diameter, keeping it only about 1cm deep. Pipe the remaining mixture into small balls, lifting off to a peak on each. Using a wet finger, gently pat down the peaks to flatten.

Place in the oven for 25 minutes until golden brown, then remove and set aside to cool. Pierce the sides of the small buns once with a small knife, and of the larger circle several times, to let the steam out.

Whisk the double cream and custard to soft peaks, then add the orange liqueur and whisk until the cream is holding its shape. Spoon one-third of the cream into a piping bag and snip the top off, creating a small nozzle.

Pierce the flat base of 16 of the small choux buns with the tips of a pair of scissors then fill with cream, piping until you feel pressure pushing back and the bun is full. (Any leftover unfilled buns freeze very well.)

Heat the sugar in a frying pan over a high heat until it forms a light golden caramel; swirl the pan, but don't stir. Quickly dip the rounded sides of the filled choux buns in the caramel to coat, then return to the tray to harden.

Place the big choux circle on a serving plate. Set two large tablespoons into hot water, then drag one at a time through the remaining cream to form small oval balls, placing on top of the choux base to cover, leaving a small border around the outside (keeping the spoons in hot water makes it easier to form quenelles).

Place the caramel-topped choux buns around the outside of the quenelles on the choux base, then decorate with the soft fruit and a few little twisted willow sprigs (if using) and serve.

RASPBERRY AND PISTACHIO TRIFLE

Who doesn't like a trifle? This one uses pistachio paste which you can now buy online and in some speciality cake shops as the popularity of cake baking continues to increase. It won't turn green; the reason commercial pistachio cakes are green is down to food colouring. The paste will give the cake a great pistachio taste, though.

Serves 6–8

For the pistachio sponge

25g unsalted butter, melted, plus more for the tin
175g plain flour, plus more for the tin
6 eggs
175g caster sugar
25g pistachio paste

For the trifle

1kg raspberries
25g flaked almonds
500ml double cream, whipped
3 tbsp icing sugar, sifted
125ml kirsch
500ml home-made vanilla custard, cooled (see page 161)
40g shelled pistachio nuts, roughly chopped

To make the sponge, preheat the oven to 200°C/400°F/gas mark 6.

Butter and flour a 23cm springform cake tin and line the base with greaseproof paper.

Place the eggs and sugar into a large bowl and whisk for about five minutes until really pale and thick, then add the pistachio paste and mix for another minute until totally incorporated.

Fold the flour and melted butter into the mixture quickly without knocking out too much air, then pour into the tin and bake for 25 minutes until golden, risen and firm.

Cool in the tin for 10 minutes, then turn out and cool on a wire rack.

To assemble the trifle, set 100g of raspberries aside, Place one-third (300g) of the remaining berries into a food processor with 2 tbsp of water. Blitz to a purée, then set aside.

Cut the cooled pistachio cake into 2cm-thick slices.

Place the flaked almonds in a small, dry frying pan and set over a medium heat. Stir until they turn a shade darker and smell toasty, then immediately tip on to a plate to stop the cooking.

Whip the cream with the icing sugar until soft peaks form.

Take a large glass serving bowl and layer in the sponge, drizzle over the kirsch, then top with some raspberry sauce, raspberries and custard, then repeat, until all the sponge, kirsch, raspberry sauce, raspberries and custard have been used up.

Top with the whipped sweetened cream, then sprinkle with the reserved 100g of raspberries, flaked almonds and chopped pistachios. Serve straight away, or chill until ready to serve.

GREENGAGE MERINGUES WITH CREAM

The good thing with this meringue is that you can make it with lots of other fruits such as cherries, raspberries, blueberries or blackberries. All the versions are just as good. I have some greengages growing in the garden at home, so that's why they are in this. The meringue turns lovely and sticky when cooked.

Serves 4

For the meringues
750g greengages, pitted and quartered
270g caster sugar
5 medium egg whites
150g icing sugar
300ml double cream
1 vanilla pod, split, seeds scraped out

Preheat the oven to 100°C/200°F/gas mark ¼.

Put 2 tbsp of water, the greengages and 120g of the caster sugar into a pan and cook for 15–20 minutes until they are soft with a sticky syrup. Remove from the heat and allow to cool totally.

Beat the egg whites in a clean bowl, using electric beaters, until the mixture forms soft peaks, then add the remaining 150g of caster sugar and beat until stiff peaks form. Sift the icing sugar over, then continue to beat until the mixture forms stiff peaks again and is really smooth and shiny.

Line a baking sheet with baking parchment, or a silicone sheet, and secure the paper with a few dabs of meringue mixture.

Fold half the cooled greengages into the meringue mixture, taking care not to knock out too much air, then place eight spoonfuls on to the baking tray.

Place into the oven and bake for two hours, then turn the oven off and open the door a bit (propping it open with a wooden spoon is a good trick). Leave the meringues to cool in the oven.

Whisk the double cream with the vanilla seeds until soft peaks form.

Spoon some of the reserved greengages into the centre of each plate. Sandwich the meringues together with the vanilla cream, set on top of the greengages and serve immediately.

BLUEBERRY STEAMED PUDDING WITH VANILLA CUSTARD

Comforting and so simple, this is food that should be cooked in every home. It's a proper pudding with proper custard. And remember it is custard, not crème anglaise.

Serves 6–8

For the pudding

175g unsalted butter, softened, plus more
  for the bowl
150g golden syrup
200g blueberries
175g golden caster sugar
3 eggs
175g self-raising flour
1 tsp baking powder
pinch of salt

For the custard

250ml whole milk
250ml double cream
1 vanilla pod, split, seeds scraped out
110g caster sugar
6 egg yolks

Start with the pudding. Butter a 1.2-litre heatproof bowl, then pour the golden syrup into the base and scatter in the blueberries.

Place the butter, sugar, eggs, flour, baking powder and a pinch of salt into a bowl and whisk until light and fluffy, then spoon carefully into the bowl.

Lay a sheet of greaseproof paper on to a sheet of foil, pleat both layers in the centre to create an overlap, then tie around the bowl with string. Take a long piece of foil and fold lengthways in half to make a handle.

Place a cloth in the base of a large saucepan, then put an upside-down saucer or small plate on it. Fill halfway up with water. Place the foil-covered bowl on to the long folded over piece of foil, then into the saucepan (this acts as a handle later to lift the pudding bowl out of the saucepan). Cover and bring to a boil, then reduce the heat and simmer for 1½–2 hours.

To make the custard, put the milk and cream into a shallow saucepan with the vanilla pod and seeds and set over a medium heat. Bring to the boil.

Meanwhile, whisk the sugar and egg yolks in a bowl. When the milk is boiling, pour it on to the eggs, whisking all the time, then return the whole mixture to the pan and cook over a gentle heat, whisking, until thick enough to coat the back of a wooden spoon. Strain into a clean pan and warm through very gently.

Use the foil strip to lift the pudding bowl out of the saucepan, then discard the foil and baking parchment. Place a plate on top and turn over, tipping the pudding on to the plate.

Cut the pudding into wedges and serve with the custard.

FAST CHOCOLATE BAR ICE CREAM WITH BLUEBERRY GALETTES

I love this. Part of the process is a bit cheffy for sure – with the Pacojet to make the ice cream – but I do it in the restaurant and at demos around the UK. The crux of this are the galettes, which are ace, simple to make and taste so good. If you don't want to spend on a fancy machine, just serve this with good bought vanilla ice cream.

Serves 8

For the chocolate bar ice cream

300ml whole milk
200ml double cream
75g caster sugar
6 egg yolks
3 chocolate and peanut bars, one end cut off

For the galettes

200g plain flour, plus more to dust
75g caster sugar
150g unsalted butter, chopped
2 egg yolks
400g blueberries
1 vanilla pod, split, seeds scraped out
2 tbsp cornflour
juice of 1 lemon
2 tbsp demerara sugar

Start with the ice cream. Heat the milk and cream in a saucepan until just simmering. Meanwhile, place the caster sugar and egg yolks into a bowl and whisk, then pour the warm milk and cream on to them, whisking all the time. Return the mixture to the saucepan and whisk until it thickens enough to coat the back of a spoon. Put in the fridge to chill.

If you're using a Pacojet, when the mixture is cold, place the chocolate bars into the container, then pour over the cold custard (it must not come up further than the 'fill here' mark on the inside of the container). Freeze for at least four hours, until frozen solid.

Or, if you do not have a Pacojet, roughly chop the chocolate bars, make the custard as above until it has thickened, then add the chocolate bars and melt into the custard. Transfer to an ice cream machine and churn until frozen, then transfer to a lidded container and freeze until needed.

Make the galettes. Put the flour, 25g of the caster sugar and the butter into a bowl and rub with your fingertips until the mixture looks like crumbs. Add one of the egg yolks and mix to form a dough. It will be quite tight, so knead until it becomes smooth. Flatten to a disc about 2cm thick, wrap in cling film and chill for 30 minutes.

Meanwhile, put the blueberries, remaining 50g of caster sugar, vanilla seeds, cornflour and lemon juice into a bowl and toss together.

Roll the pastry out on a lightly floured surface to 5mm thick, then stamp out eight 12cm discs and pull the sides up to form little pastry cases. Transfer to a large baking sheet lined with baking parchment, then fill with the blueberries. Brush the pastry with the remaining egg yolk, then sprinkle over the demerara. Place in the fridge for 30 minutes to firm up. Preheat the oven to 200°C/400°F/gas mark 6.

Bake the galettes in the oven for 25 minutes until deep golden and crispy.

Place the container into the Pacojet and blitz to form ice cream, or remove the churned ice cream from the freezer to soften slightly. Spoon the ice cream on to the warm galettes and serve straight away.

HOME-MADE WAFFLES WITH STRAWBERRY COMPOTE

You will need a waffle maker for this recipe. I never knew how simple waffles were to make, or how quick, before I used one. I've only used strawberries because I have bucket-loads of them in my garden; other fruits such as raspberries and apricots would be just as good.

Serves 4

For the waffles

250g plain flour
1½ tsp baking powder
1 tsp salt
1 tbsp caster sugar
3 free-range eggs, lightly beaten
425ml whole milk
110g unsalted butter, melted, plus more for the waffle maker

For the strawberry compote

75g caster sugar
25g unsalted butter
250g strawberries, hulled
finely grated zest of 1 unwaxed lemon
500ml vanilla ice cream, to serve
4–8 tbsp maple syrup, to serve

For the waffles, preheat a waffle maker to a medium setting and preheat the oven to 140°C/275°F/gas mark 1.

Mix the flour, baking powder, salt and sugar in a large mixing bowl. Whisk in the eggs, milk and butter.

Butter the waffle maker lightly, then ladle some of the batter into each well of the waffle maker, close the lid and cook for five minutes, or until golden-brown and crispy. Remove and place on a tray in the oven to keep warm while you cook the rest.

To make the compote, place the sugar and 75ml of water with the butter into a small sauté pan, then add the strawberries and lemon zest and simmer for five minutes.

Stack the waffles on to a plate, top with some strawberry compote and a dollop of vanilla ice cream. Finish with a drizzle of maple syrup.

HOME-MADE MARSHMALLOWS
WITH CHOCOLATE SAUCE

I remember when I was a kid that Flumps were the sweet of choice for me. But, these days, they're hard to find. So now for parties at mine I make this. It really is easy, a marshmallow is basically just a meringue with gelatine and that's about it.

Serves 450g

For the marshmallows

450g granulated sugar

1 tbsp liquid glucose

9 sheets of gelatine

2 large egg whites

1 tsp vanilla extract

2 tbsp flavourless vegetable oil, for the baking tray

5–6 tbsp icing sugar, to dust

5–6 tbsp cornflour, to dust

For the chocolate sauce

75g caster sugar

200g dark chocolate, roughly chopped

To make the meringues, place the granulated sugar, glucose and 200ml of water into a heavy-based saucepan and bring to the boil. Cook over a medium-high heat until a sugar thermometer shows 127°C/260°F. Meanwhile, soak the gelatine in 140ml of water. Add the soaked gelatine sheets and their soaking water to the hot sugar syrup very carefully. Stir to dissolve, then pour into a jug.

Place the egg whites into a clean grease-free bowl and whisk to firm peaks. Continuing to whisk, pour the sugar syrup on to the egg whites, until the mixture is shiny.

Add the vanilla extract and continue to whisk for five to 10 minutes until the mixture is thick enough to hold its shape on a whisk.

Lightly oil a 30 x 20cm baking tray.

Dust the tray with icing sugar and cornflour then spoon in the marshmallow, smoothing the top with a wet palette knife. Place in the fridge for at least one hour to set.

Dust some more icing sugar and cornflour over a work surface. Loosen the edge of the marshmallow, then turn out on to the work surface. Cut into squares and roll in the icing sugar and cornflour to coat totally.

For the chocolate sauce, place the sugar and 110ml of water into a saucepan and bring to a simmer. Cook for one or two minutes until all the sugar has dissolved, then add the chocolate. Whisk until smooth, then remove from the heat.

Carefully thread the marshmallows on to skewers. Place on a hot griddle, under a grill, over an open fire or into a tandoor and grill for one or two minutes until a bit charred and gooey.

Serve the skewers of marshmallows with a bowl of chocolate sauce.

CHOCOLATE TRUFFLES

Saves buying them and means you can flavour the truffles with whatever you wish. The key is not to use chocolate that is too rich or that has too high a cocoa solid content as, to me, it doesn't taste as good. Still, buy the best-quality chocolate you can afford for these.

Serves 6–8

350ml double cream
400g 60% cocoa solids dark chocolate, broken into pieces
3–4 tbsp sifted cocoa powder

Pour the cream into a saucepan and bring to the boil. Put the chocolate into a bowl, then pour over the boiling cream and mix well until the mixture is smooth.

Set aside to cool, then cover and place into the fridge to chill and become firm for about two hours.

Sift the cocoa powder on to a plate and, using a teaspoon, curl balls of chocolate and drop straight into the cocoa, then roll to coat,

Place on a clean plate to firm up, then serve, or keep in a sealed container in the fridge for up to four weeks.

HONEYCOMB

This is so easy to make. The trick is to cook the sugar and cool it for a minute before whisking in the bicarb. That way the mix will rise and stay up. If the bicarb is added too soon, the bubbles burst and the mix collapses as it cools.

Serves 6–8

200g caster sugar
50ml runny honey
1 tbsp liquid glucose
¾ tsp bicarbonate of soda

Place the sugar, honey, glucose and 50ml of water into a saucepan and bring to the boil. Continue to cook until the temperature reaches 160°C/320°F on a sugar thermometer.

Remove from the heat, allow to cool for 30 seconds so the bubbles disperse, then quickly beat in the bicarbonate of soda, stirring constantly.

Pour on to a silicone-lined baking sheet and leave to cool for 30 minutes.

Break into shards and store in a sealed container until you want to serve it. It will keep well for up to one week.

INSTANT COFFEE MERINGUE GÂTEAU

You might not think, looking at it, that you could do this or that it's easy… but I proved the camera crew on the photoshoot wrong. It's not for the diet conscious, but my desserts never are. Using bought meringues and marshmallows saves masses of time. I hope you like it as much as the crew did. They're all on the treadmill now, mind…

Serves 6–8

For the gateau
6 medium egg whites
200g caster sugar
100g icing sugar, sifted
2 tbsp coffee essence
500g mascarpone cheese
175ml double cream
1 vanilla pod, split, seeds scraped out
2 x 250g large sponge flan cases
175ml cold espresso

To serve
10 small meringue shells
2 tbsp cocoa powder
4 marshmallows, quartered
1 tsp icing sugar
50g dark chocolate, finely grated

Place the egg whites in a large clean bowl and whisk until the mixture forms stiff peaks. Add the caster and icing sugars and continue to beat for about five minutes, until the mixture is smooth and shiny. Beat in the coffee essence, then set aside.

Beat the mascarpone, cream and vanilla seeds together until smooth.

Use a 20cm ring to stamp out the centres of the flan cases, then cut each disc of sponge in half horizontally.

Place the ring on to a serving plate, then lay one piece of cake into it, brush over one-quarter of the cold coffee, then spread over one-third of the mascarpone mixture.

Repeat with the remaining cake and sponge; you will have four layers of sponge and three layers of cream.

Dollop most of the coffee meringue on top, spread it roughly around the sides of the cake, then sear with a kitchen blowtorch until light golden brown.

Dust the meringues with the cocoa powder, then stick each on to a marshmallow piece with a little of the coffee meringue. Place on top of the cake in a little cluster. Dust with icing sugar and grated chocolate, then serve.

baked comforts

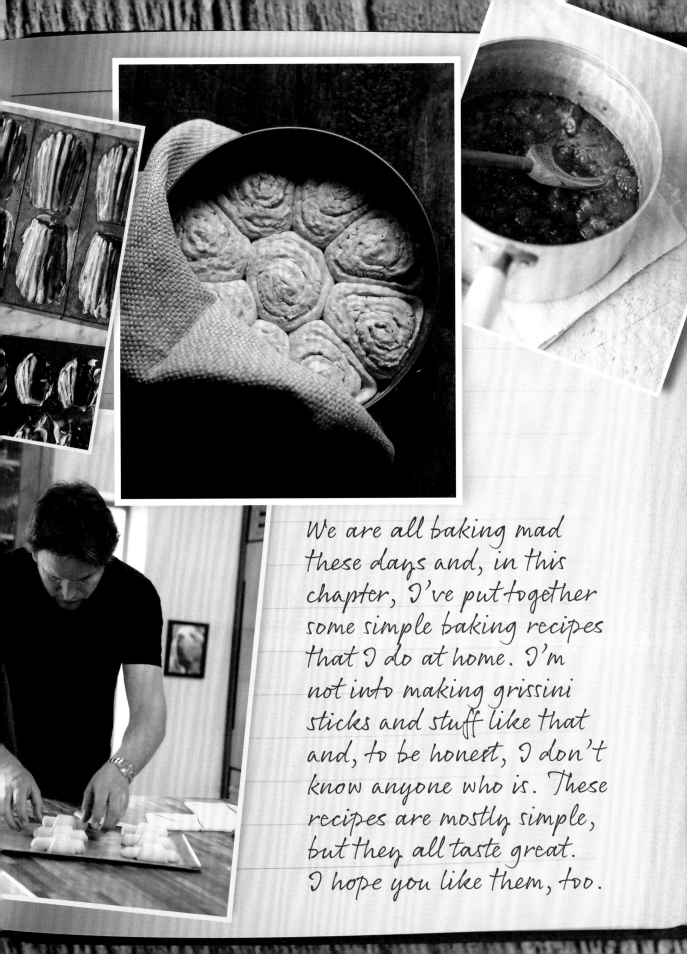

We are all baking mad these days and, in this chapter, I've put together some simple baking recipes that I do at home. I'm not into making grissini sticks and stuff like that and, to be honest, I don't know anyone who is. These recipes are mostly simple, but they all taste great. I hope you like them, too.

THE BEST CINNAMON ROLLS

God knows how many calories this has in it; I certainly don't but – believe me – someone out there will and I'll get letters! To those people who don't care, you can serve this with toffee sauce and vanilla ice cream. Just enjoy these for what they are, as the flavours are off the scale. You need good-quality flour to bake great cinnamon rolls and NR Stoate & Sons, the Dorset mill we visited on the TV show, is a great example of the artisan millers which are popping up all over the country.

Serves 6 – 8

For the dough
625g strong white bread flour, plus more to dust
75g caster sugar
pinch of sea salt
20g fast-action dried yeast
500g cold unsalted butter, plus more for the tin

For the filling
300g full-fat cream cheese
1 vanilla pod, split, seeds scraped out
1 tsp ground cinnamon
2 egg yolks, lightly beaten

For the glaze
200g icing sugar, sifted
100ml maple syrup
25ml bourbon whiskey

For the dough, place the flour, sugar, salt and yeast into a mixer fitted with a dough hook and slowly mix in about 450ml of water, adding more or less as needed to make a dough. Process until it starts sticking to the edge of the bowl and feels elastic.

Turn off the machine, lift out the hook and cover the bowl with a tea towel. Leave it in a warm place for the dough to rise for about 20 minutes, or until doubled in size. Now knock the air out of it and roll out on a floured surface into a rectangle measuring 60 x 30cm.

Slice the butter 1cm thick and arrange over half the dough, lengthways, leaving a border. Fold the other half of the dough over and press down lightly at the edges to seal in the butter.

On a well-floured surface, beat the dough with the rolling pin, then roll into a 60 x 30cm rectangle again. Fold one short side over by one-third, then the other short side on top of it, as though you were folding a business letter. Repeat the rolling, beating and folding process three times. Wrap the dough in cling film and leave to rest in the fridge for one hour.

Roll the dough out into a rectangle about 1cm thick.

For the filling, mix the cream cheese, vanilla seeds and cinnamon. Cover the dough with the mixture, then roll up from a longer side. Cut into slices about 5cm thick.

Butter and line a 23cm springform tin. Place the slices, cut-sides up, around the edge and one in the middle, making sure they are not too tightly packed. Leave in a warm place to prove until doubled in size; it should take about 40 minutes.

When ready to bake, preheat the oven to 200°C/400°F/gas mark 6. Brush the dough with the beaten egg and bake for 45 minutes until golden brown.

While the rolls are cooling slightly, make the glaze by mixing the icing sugar, maple syrup and bourbon together until smooth.

Lift the 'cake' of rolls out of the tin and set on a serving plate, then drizzle the glaze over the top, back and forth. Leave to set. Tear off the rolls to serve.

GINGER PARKIN
WITH RHUBARB
AND SPICED SYRUP

This is best when made in advance and kept in an airtight tin for two or three days, as it will become really sticky all the way through.

Serves 8

For the parkin

150g softened unsalted butter,
  plus more for the tin
150g soft light brown sugar
250g golden syrup
75g black treacle
125g rolled oats
175g self-raising flour
3 tbsp ground ginger
1 tsp ground nutmeg
1 tsp mixed spice
pinch of salt
2 eggs, lightly beaten
25ml milk

For the rhubarb

50g unsalted butter
75g caster sugar
finely grated zest of 1 orange
4 rhubarb sticks, cut into 5cm lengths

For the sauce

200g golden syrup
100ml dry cider
½ tsp mixed spice
½ tsp ground ginger
¼ tsp ground nutmeg

For the parkin, preheat the oven to 140°C/275°F/gas mark 1 and butter a 30 x 20cm cake tin.

Put the 150g of butter, soft brown sugar, syrup and treacle into a small saucepan and melt over a gentle heat. Tip the oats, flour, spices and salt into a bowl, mix together, then add the eggs and milk. Pour the contents of the saucepan on to the flour mixture and stir together with a whisk until combined.

Pour into the prepared tin and bake for 1¼ hours, or until firm to the touch in the centre.

Remove from the oven and leave in the tin to cool before turning out. When cold, store in an airtight tin, ideally for a couple of days.

To cook the rhubarb, put the butter, sugar and 75ml of water into a sauté pan with the orange zest and rhubarb and set over a gentle heat to poach for four or five minutes until just tender, then remove from the heat.

For the sauce, place the syrup, cider and spices into a saucepan and bring to the boil, then cook for three or four minutes until just thickened.

Cut the parkin into squares and place them on plates. Spoon the rhubarb to one side and pour a little syrup over the top. Serve with vanilla ice cream, if you like (for a home-made recipe, see page 152).

There are lemon tarts and lemon tarts. Good versions, like the one you should be able to produce with this recipe, are good enough to grace Michelin three-star restaurant menus. It is a true test of any cook. Get it right and it's the best dessert in the world. Get it wrong and not only will it taste rubbish, it will leak all over the oven and take two days to clean up. The pastry must be thin and cooked through; if it's too thick it will not taste nice. But the real trick is in the oven temperature and knowing when your tart is just done: overcook it and the filling will crack and split; have the oven too hot and the mixture will soufflé up and separate; have the oven too cool and the pastry will go soft and leak. Good luck!

Serves 6–8

For the pastry
250g plain flour, plus more to dust
100g cold unsalted butter, chopped,
  plus more for the tart ring
25g icing sugar
pinch of salt
1 egg, lightly beaten

For the filling
14 eggs
550g caster sugar
700ml double cream
finely grated zest and juice of 10 large
  unwaxed lemons
icing sugar, to glaze
crème fraîche, to serve

To make the pastry, put the flour, butter, icing sugar and salt into a bowl and rub with your fingertips until it has the texture of fine crumbs. Add the egg and mix together until it forms a dough, then knead lightly on a board until smooth. Roll into a ball, wrap in cling film and put in the fridge to rest for 30 minutes.

Meanwhile, preheat the oven to 160°C/325°F/gas mark 3. Make the filling: break the eggs into a bowl, add the sugar, cream, lemon zest and juice and whisk. Strain through a fine sieve, then cover and refrigerate.

Roll the pastry out on a work surface lightly dusted with flour to about 3mm thick. Keep turning the pastry a quarter turn every time you roll it, so you end up with a perfect circle.

Butter the inside of a 25cm, 4.5cm-deep tart ring and a baking sheet. Place the ring on the sheet, then line it with the pastry, carefully lifting the pastry then pressing it into the base, so it hangs over the edge. Line with several sheets of ovenproof cling film or one sheet of baking parchment to hang over by 10cm, then fill with flour, baking beans or raw rice. Fold the cling film or baking parchment back over that and bake for 15 minutes.

Remove the cling film or parchment and its contents, brush the inside of the tart with the beaten egg and return to the oven for another three or four minutes until just golden.

Reduce the oven temperature to 150°C/300°F/gas mark 2.

Skim any bubbles from the top of the filling and discard. Remove the tart from the oven, add half the filling, then transfer to the oven shelf. Now pull the oven shelf out and ladle the rest of the filling in, then carefully push the tray back into the oven and bake for one hour. (This lessens the risk of spilling the filling all over the floor!) Remove when it still just wobbles in the centre, then leave to cool to room temperature.

To serve, cut the tart into wedges and dust with icing sugar, then glaze either under the grill or with a blowtorch. Serve with crème fraîche.

I have masses of lavender in my garden (that's some of it you can see to the left!) and cook it with lamb as well as in this pudding.

The key to using lavender in cooking is not to use too much, or it can overpower food and make it taste like your auntie's soap.

Serves 6

For the crème caramel

225g caster sugar

150ml whole milk

300ml double cream

½–1 tbsp dried lavender tips (check the strength first!)

4 eggs, lightly beaten

For the lavender shortbread

175g unsalted butter, softened, plus more for the tin

100g icing sugar

½–1 tbsp dried lavender tips (check the strength first!)

100g cornflour

200g plain flour

2 tbsp caster sugar (optional)

Place six 7.5cm diameter, 4cm-deep ramekins into a deep roasting tray. Preheat the oven to 150°C/300°F/gas mark 2.

Put 150g of the caster sugar into a saucepan over a high heat and cook without stirring until a golden brown caramel, swirling the pan from time to time. Remove the pan from the heat and carefully add 2 tbsp of hot water; it will spit and splutter a little but swirl to combine, then divide equally between the ramekins and roll around the sides to coat evenly.

Place the milk, cream and lavender into a saucepan and heat gently until just simmering. Meanwhile, put the eggs and remaining 75g of the sugar into a bowl and whisk until combined, then pour on the simmering milk, whisking constantly, until smooth. Strain the custard through a fine sieve into the ramekins and half-fill the roasting tray with hot water so that the water comes two-thirds of the way up the sides of the ramekins.

Carefully place in the oven and bake for 45 minutes until just set, then remove. Allow to cool to room temperature, then remove the ramekins from the tin and chill in the fridge for at least one hour.

Make the shortbread. Preheat the oven to 180°C/350°F/gas mark 4 and butter a 30 x 20cm baking tin.

Put the butter and icing sugar into a bowl and beat until light and fluffy, with an electric whisk if you like, then fold in the lavender, cornflour and plain flour and mix to a firm dough. Press into the tin to lie about 1cm thick, prick all over with a fork and scatter the caster sugar over the top (if using).

Bake in the oven for 12–15 minutes until light golden brown and cooked through. Leave to cool briefly in the tin, then break into shards.

To remove the crème caramels from the ramekins, run a knife around each, then press the knife lightly into one side, before inverting on to plates. Serve with the shortbread.

HOME-MADE
BUTTERY CROISSANTS

If you ever wondered what goes into making a croissant… well, now you know: a fair bit of elbow grease. But the rewards are great. Good-quality butter is a must for this and that's why the French croissants taste so good. The butter needs to be cold and firm. (You can't make these with margarine, before you dare to ask!) You need to start these the day before you want them.

Once you've shaped the croissants, you can place them in the fridge, cover and bake them when you need. They keep for about 12 hours just fine.

Makes 16

625g strong white bread flour, plus more to dust
75g caster sugar
12g fine sea salt
40g fresh yeast
500g unsalted butter, chilled
1 egg and 1 egg yolk, lightly beaten

The day before you want to bake the croissants, place the flour, sugar, salt and yeast in a food mixer fitted with a dough hook, or a large mixing bowl, add 350–400ml of water and mix to a soft dough. Tip on to a floured work surface and knead really well until it feels elastic, then set aside.

Place the chilled butter between two sheets of greaseproof paper and bash flat with a rolling pin to a 30 x 20cm rectangle about 1cm thick. Place in the fridge while you roll out the dough.

Lift the dough back out on to a floured surface and roll out to a large rectangle, about 60 x 30cm.

Put the butter in the centre of the dough and fold one side of the dough over the butter, then fold the other side over to meet it, covering the butter. Fold it all in half lengthways.

Turn 90°, then roll out again to a 60 x 30cm rectangle. Fold one-quarter of the dough across to the centre, then fold the other side over to meet it. Fold it in half lengthways, then repeat the whole process twice more. Fold over, then cover and place in the fridge to rest overnight.

Roll the dough out to 5mm thick, then cut into two 50 x 20cm strips. Cut each strip into triangles about 10cm wide at the base.

Place a dough triangle with the narrow point facing away from you, then stretch the bottom points out sideways. Roll it over itself and curl it into a traditional crescent shape. Repeat to shape all the croissants.

Place on baking trays lined with silicone paper, brush with egg and leave to rise for 30–45 minutes. They can be frozen at this point, or left in the fridge overnight to prove.

When ready to bake, preheat the oven to 190°C/375°F/gas mark 5. Bake for 25 minutes until golden brown.

BRAMLEY MARZIPAN SLICE

This is so simple to make. You can even use ready-made Bramley apple sauce, would you believe. But whether bought or home-made, the apple sauce must be made with Bramleys as it's their sharpness combined with the sweet marzipan that makes this work so well.

Serves 4 – 6

750g Bramley apples, peeled, cored and roughly chopped
50–75g caster sugar
25g unsalted butter, plus more for the tray
2 x 320g all-butter puff pastry sheets (about 35 x 23cm)
250g natural marzipan, thinly sliced
2 egg yolks, lightly beaten
2 tbsp demerara sugar
200g clotted cream, to serve

Preheat the oven to 200°C/400°F/gas mark 6.

Place the apples and the smaller amount of caster sugar into a saucepan with the butter and 3 tbsp of water. Bring to the boil, cover and cook for three to five minutes until the apple has softened. Remove the lid and stir to combine, then cook for another two or three minutes until totally softened and purée-like. Taste to see if it needs the rest of the caster sugar. If it does, stir it in while the purée is hot, so it dissolves. Remove from the heat and allow to cool.

Put one of the sheets of pastry on a buttered baking tray and lay the slices of marzipan over, leaving a border of 2cm all the way around, then spread the cooled apple purée over the marzipan. Brush some of the beaten egg yolks around the pastry border.

Fold the second sheet of puff pastry in half lengthways and carefully slice through from the fold towards the edges at 1cm intervals down the length of the pastry, making sure to leave 2cm intact at the edges.

Unfold and you will have a piece of puff pastry that has a 2cm border and the centre sliced. Lay this on top of the apple-covered pastry, making sure that it sits directly over, crimp the edges, then trim them so they are straight.

Brush with the remaining egg yolks and scatter the demerara over the top. Bake in the oven for 30 minutes until golden brown and crispy.

Serve warm with the clotted cream.

APPLE AND BLACKBERRY MILLEFEUILLE TART

There are few desserts that look as impressive as a millefeuille and it's a favourite of my old mate, the top chef Pierre Koffmann. Making your own puff pastry is ideal as it will taste far better, though I admit it is more time-consuming. And let's face it, if you had one of the world's greatest chefs coming round for dinner, what would you do? Panic. Well you're not alone, as I still do that!

Serves 8–10

For the rough puff pastry

250g plain flour, plus more to dust
250g very cold butter, cut into small cubes
½ tsp salt
25g icing sugar

For the rest

40g unsalted butter
2 large Bramley apples, peeled, cored and roughly chopped
1 vanilla pod, split, seeds scraped out
juice of 1 lemon
125g blackberries
300ml double cream

For the pastry, place the flour in a mound on a clean work surface and make a well in the centre.

Place the butter and salt in the well and work them together with the fingertips of one hand, gradually drawing the flour into the centre with the other hand. When the cubes of butter have become small pieces and the dough looks grainy, gradually add 125ml of ice-cold water and mix until it is all incorporated. Don't overwork the dough; you should have a marbled effect with the butter; on this occasion it shouldn't be mixed in totally.

Roll the mixture out on a lightly floured surface into a 2.5cm-thick rectangle, wrap in cling film and refrigerate for 20 minutes.

Flour the work surface and roll out the pastry into a 40 x 20cm rectangle. Fold one short side over by one-third, then the other short side on top of it, as though you were folding a business letter. Turn 90°. Roll the pastry into a 40 x 20cm rectangle as before and fold into three again. These are the first two turns. Wrap in cling film and chill for 15–30 minutes. Repeat twice more to make four turns in total.

Wrap in cling film and chill for at least 30 minutes before using.

Preheat the oven to 220°C/425°F/gas mark 7. Roll the pastry out on a lightly floured surface to a 22.5 x 15cm rectangle about 3mm thick, then cut into three rectangles, each 15 x 7.5cm. Dredge two of them with icing sugar, to cover. Lift on to a baking tray and bake for 15 minutes.

Meanwhile, make the filling. Heat a small sauté pan until hot, add the butter and apples and cook for a minute, then add 2–3 tbsp of water and continue to cook. Add the vanilla pod and seeds, lemon juice and blackberries and cook for five or six minutes until softened and pulpy. Allow to cool, then chill in the fridge.

Whisk the double cream to firm peaks, then spoon into a piping bag.

Slice the cooled pastry sheets in half horizontally through the depth of the pastry; you will now have six very thin rectangles. Set aside the two glazed pieces for the tops.

Spoon some of the blackberry mix on a piece of pastry, then pipe the cream over. Place another piece of pastry on top then repeat with another layer of blackberry and cream. Finish with an icing sugar-glazed piece of pastry. Repeat to make another millefeuille. Serve immediately.

FRANGIPANE TARTS WITH HOME-MADE CUSTARD

Still one of my favourite recipes to cook at home and, in fact, one of my favourite recipes in this book. You can make one big or eight small tarts but, in either case, don't overfill the tins as the mixture rises and expands and, importantly, never refrigerate the cooked tarts as the frangipane will set hard and they will end up tasting like shop-bought versions. Not that they will even make it to the fridge; they taste too good.

Serves 8

For the pastry
125g cold unsalted butter, chopped
250g plain flour, plus more to dust
1 egg, lightly beaten

For the filling
225g raspberry jam
225g unsalted butter, softened
1 vanilla pod, split, seeds scraped out
225g caster sugar
5 eggs
225g ground almonds
75g whole blanched almonds

For the custard
250ml milk
250ml double cream
110g caster sugar
4 egg yolks

For the pastry, put the butter and flour into a food mixer and pulse-blend until it looks like crumbs, then add the egg and mix until it forms a firm dough. Wrap in cling film and put in the fridge to rest for 30 minutes.

To make the tart, roll the pastry out to about 3mm thick on to a work surface lightly dusted with flour.

Carefully line eight 10cm loose-bottomed tart tins, or a 23cm deep-sided loose-bottomed tart tin, with the pastry, pressing it into the edges. Spread the jam over the base or bases, then leave to rest in the fridge for 10 minutes. Preheat the oven to 180°C/350°F/gas mark 4.

For the filling, beat the butter, vanilla seeds and sugar together in a bowl until pale and fluffy (save the empty vanilla pod). Crack in the eggs, one at a time, beating well after each addition, until they have all been fully incorporated. Carefully fold in the ground almonds.

Spread the filling over the jam, smoothing it to the edges, then decorate with the almonds, in concentric circles.

Place the tart or tarts in the oven and cook for 25 minutes for the tartlets or 35–40 minutes for the large tart, or until the filling has risen and is cooked through and the surface is an even pale golden-brown.

Make the custard as on page 161, but without the vanilla seeds (just use the empty pod).

To serve, cut the tart into wedges or place a tartlet on a plate and pour the custard alongside.

SWISS ROLL WITH
FRESH RASPBERRY JAM

Having this recipe in a book will have my chef mates laughing… but trust me, if this was on a dessert buffet it would be the first one they would go for. I grow my own soft fruit in my garden – the raspberry plants come from Scotland, the home of the best raspberries in the world – and this is the perfect way to use up what I have left. It's not a jam recipe as you know it; this is quicker to make and will do nicely. Let the sponge cool fully before rolling and, if the tea towel you use to roll it up is damp, it shouldn't crack.

Serves 6

For the jam
450g raspberries
400g jam sugar

For the sponge
5 eggs
125g caster sugar, plus more to dust
2 vanilla pods, split, seeds scraped out
95g self-raising flour
500ml double cream
75g raspberries
8 tiny sprigs of mint or lemon verbena
1 tbsp chopped pistachio nuts (optional)

Make the raspberry jam first. Place a large saucepan on the heat with the raspberries, sugar and 3 tbsp of water and cook gently for two to three minutes until the sugar has dissolved. Increase the heat and cook for a further six or seven minutes until just thick enough to coat the back of a spoon. Remove from the heat, pour into hot, sterilised jars (see page 21) and cool.

For the sponge, preheat the oven to 190°C/375°F/gas mark 5 and line a 38 x 25cm Swiss roll tin with a sheet of baking parchment.

Place the eggs, sugar and the seeds from one of the vanilla pods into a bowl and whisk until very light, fluffy and thickened. Sift the flour over the mixture and fold it in with your hand; carefully lifting and mixing until it is all incorporated.

Pour into the lined tin and smooth with a spatula until evenly spread out. Bake for 10–12 minutes, or until just firm to the touch.

Place a damp, wrung-out tea towel that is slightly bigger than the Swiss roll tin on a work surface and dust it with caster sugar. Turn the sponge out on to the tea towel, then peel off the parchment on the bottom of the sponge. Starting at the longest edge nearest you, roll the sponge up in the tea towel, pressing gently as you go, then unroll and allow to cool.

When you're ready to assemble the dish, whip the double cream and remaining vanilla seeds to firm peaks.

Spread the raspberry jam over the cooled sponge, leaving a 2cm border at the furthest long edge.

Spread most of the whipped cream over the top, then, taking the longest edge and using the tea towel to help, roll up the sponge quite tightly, making sure the filling stays inside.

Roll the sponge off the tea towel on to a serving plate and dust with more caster sugar.

Serve with the raspberries and sprigs of mint or lemn verbena. If you like – and are feeling flash – you can make 'quenelles' of leftover cream with two hot spoons, to decorate the Swiss roll, or sprinkle it with pistachios.

CINNAMON MADELEINES WITH WINTER-SPICED CARAMEL SAUCE

A classic from France, madeleines need the correct moulds. Mine are old tins I ended up buying on an auction site, but you can get new tins that work better. The batter can be made, covered and stored in the fridge before cooking for up to one day, as the key to these is to bake and serve them on the same day. I've done a nice twist on a caramel sauce here, but they are just as good with chocolate sauce (for a recipe, see page 165).

Don't overfill the madeleine tins or they will come out shapeless; you want the pretty shell-like shape here.

Serves 4–6

For the madeleines

225g unsalted butter, plus more for the tin(s)
250g caster sugar, plus 75g to dust
250g plain flour
1 vanilla pod, split, seeds scraped out
2 tbsp runny honey
3 eggs, lightly beaten
½ tsp ground cinnamon

For the sauce

100g caster sugar
350ml double cream
1 star anise
½ cinnamon stick
25g unsalted butter

To make the madeleines, preheat the oven to 160°C/325°F/gas mark 3 and butter the madeleine tins. If you've only got one madeleine tin (more likely!), just bake them in batches.

Gently heat the butter in a saucepan until just melted.

Mix the sugar and flour in a bowl, then add the vanilla seeds (reserve the pod), honey and eggs. Whisk in the melted butter until you have a nice smooth batter. Spoon into the tins, only half filling each indent.

Bake for 12–15 minutes for larger madeleines, or eight to 10 minutes for smaller, depending on your tin.

While the madeleines are still warm, place the sugar for dusting in a broad, shallow dish with the ground cinnamon. Roll them around to coat. The madeleines can be kept in an airtight container for up to one week.

For the sauce, place the sugar into a pan and heat until a light golden brown. Don't stir the pan, but swirl it occasionally. Pour in half the cream and bring to the boil, stirring well.

Add the star anise, cinnamon, reserved vanilla pod and butter, then pour in the remaining cream and cook for two or three minutes until thickened and smooth. Strain through a fine sieve into a serving bowl.

Serve the madeleines with the sauce.

Index

First big thanks must go to Damian Kavanagh and Carla Maria Lawson at the BBC whose idea the series was. Cheers to Karen Plumb whose brains put it all together, for making it make sense and to her and the crew for turning my driveway into what looked like a Glastonbury camp site for four weeks. Thanks to all the guys at Quadrille also for making my kitchen look like a Glastonbury camp site for a further four weeks. Cheers to Janet, David and Chris for helping with the cooking and putting my house back to normal. And to my hounds Fudge and Ralph who enjoyed the TV show more than anyone, thanks to the bits of food falling on the floor.